25 Mountain Bike Tours
in Massachusetts

Mountain Bike Tours
in Massachusetts

From the Connecticut River
to the Atlantic Coast

Robert S. Morse

Photographs by the author

25 Mountain Bike Tours™ Guide

Backcountry Publications
Woodstock, Vermont

An Invitation to the Reader

Although it is unlikely that the roads you cycle on these tours will change much with time, some road signs, landmarks, and other items may. If you find that changes have occurred on these routes, please let us know so we may correct future editions. The author and publisher also welcome other comments and suggestions. Address all correspondence to:

Editor
Backcountry Publications
P.O. Box 748
Woodstock, Vermont 05091

Library of Congress Cataloging-in-Publication Data

Morse, Robert S.
  25 mountain bike tours in Massachusetts : from the Connecticut
River to the Atlantic Coast / Robert S. Morse ; photographs by the
author.
      p.   cm.
  "A 25 mountain bike tours guide."
  ISBN 0–88150–191–3 :
  1. All-terrain cycling—Massachusetts—Boston Metropolitan Area—
Guide-books. 2. All terrain cycling—Massachusetts—Guide-books.
3. Boston Metropolitan Area (Mass.)—Description—Guide-books.
4. Massachusetts—Description and travel—1981- —Guide-books.
I. Title.   II. Title: Twenty-five mountain bike tours in
Massachusetts from the Connecticut River to the Atlantic Coast.
GV1045.5.M42B675   1991
796.6'4'0974461—dc20   91–15374
                                                            CIP

Published by Backcountry Publications, a division of Countryman Press
PO Box 748, Woodstock, VT 05091
Distributed by W.W. Norton & Company, Inc.
500 Fifth Avenue, New York, NY 10110

Printed in the United States of America
Typesetting by The Sant Bani Press
Cover design, layout and paste-up by VLS Designs
Text design by Richard Widhu
Maps by Richard Widhu, © 1991 The Countryman Press

Cover photograph by Virginia Scott
All interior photographs by the Author

Acknowledgments

To acknowledge the many people who deserve thanks for helping with this book, I must start at the beginning and thank my Dad, Merton Morse, who taught me to ride a bike many years ago. As my Dad was teaching me to ride my family was there cheering me on, and they were still there cheering as I wrote this book. Thanks go to Sandy, Jim, Sue, Emma, Diane, Meg and Doug for their encouragement throughout this project.

For introducing me to the sport of mountain biking I must thank Paul Heller. Without his contagious enthusiasm for the sport, I might today still be riding only on the roads. Thanks also go to my friends and comrades-on-wheels, Paul Hennemeyer, Mark Mendel and Steve Stroubakis, with whom I have enjoyed many a midnight ride and off-road mudbath, and to Laurie Heller, whose gracious country home hospitality made many a mountain biking weekend possible.

The production of this book was a group effort with many people helping out along the way. Thanks to Carl Taylor, who kept the project moving from beginning to end; Sarah Spiers, whose insightful comments guided me throughout; Doris Safie, whose attention to detail sharpened many a paragraph; Clare Innes, who pulled the final product together; Anne Clemens, who kept our business moving while I was out on the trails and lent her editorial talents to the text; and Meg Hetfield, who provided advice on the book's design and layout. Thanks also to the many people who posed for photos, including Tammy Beaulieu, Joyce Gagnon, Sue Lennon, Gary Souza and Ted Vansant, to Dave and Phyllis Smith, who provided a home-away-from-home in Central Massachusetts, and to all who test rode chapters, including Greg Boland, Kyle Gates, Mike McCabe, Bob Mihalek, Steve Offiler, and Sonia Townsend, as well as many unnamed others.

Special thanks go to Andrea Smith, who rode with me through thick and thin, rescued me when I was lost, and advised, supported, and encouraged me at every turn.

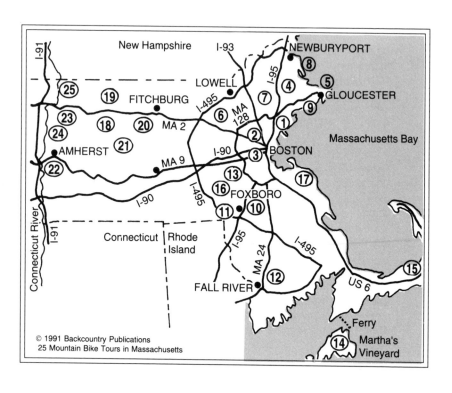

New Hampshire

I-93

NEWBURYPORT

I-91

LOWELL

I-95

GLOUCESTER

㉕   ⑲   FITCHBURG   I-495

㉓   ⑱   ⑳   MA 2

㉔   ㉑

AMHERST   MA 9

⑥   MA 128   ⑦   ④   ⑤   ⑧

②   ①   ⑨

Massachusetts Bay

I-90   ③   BOSTON

㉒   I-90   ⑬   ⑰

⑯   FOXBORO

⑪   ⑩

I-91   Connecticut | Rhode Island

Connecticut River   I-495

I-95   MA 24   I-495

FALL RIVER   ⑫   US 6   ⑮

Ferry

⑭   Martha's Vineyard

© 1991 Backcountry Publications
25 Mountain Bike Tours in Massachusetts

Contents

Introduction

In the past few years, the sport of mountain biking has exploded in popularity as more people discover the pleasures of riding a bicycle off-road. The reasons for the sport's growth are simple: mountain biking combines the freedom of riding a bicycle with the enjoyment of being outdoors, away from traffic. People are coming to the sport from all directions: road bikers escaping the noise and congestion of the streets for the quiet solitude of the woods; hikers learning to appreciate the easy access to the backcountry a bike can provide; racers seeking the challenge of maneuvering a bike along a rocky trail; and recreational riders, who simply enjoy the fun of riding a bicycle through the woods.

For whatever reason they come to the sport, every mountain biker faces the same question: Where to ride? There are many fine places to ride off-road in Massachusetts, but because mountain biking is still a relatively new sport, many of them are not well known. The sixth smallest state, Massachusetts has the sixth largest system of state parks and forests, comprising over 250,000 acres in 150 separate properties. Add to this the countless acres of public and privately owned reservations, town conservation land, watershed areas, municipal parks and the miles of old dirt roads, fire roads and bridle paths that crisscross the state, and you have a multitude of off-road riding opportunities. Many of these spots are hidden gems, known only to the people living in the towns around them. Others are well known to hikers and horseback riders but haven't yet been discovered by mountain bikers. This book provides an introduction to the diversity of trails across the state that are accessible to mountain bikers.

Besides being a guide to new riding areas, there is another important facet to this book. The sport of mountain biking today is at the center of a nationwide controversy over trail access. Some people believe that riding a bike off-road is damaging to the environment, dangerous to other trail users, and an intrusion on the quality of the wilderness experience. Educating mountain bikers on the ethic of "soft cycling" — riding off-road in a responsible, safe and environmentally sound way — is the key to alleviating this controversy. Thus, the principles of safe and responsible riding are laid out in this Introduction and reemphasized where appropriate in each chapter. Restrictions regarding the use of mountain bikes in particular areas are clearly spelled out. As much as possible, tour routes have been chosen to minimize encounters with hikers and equestrians. And finally, by showing many people new places to ride, it is hoped that this book will serve to distribute ridership over a wider choice of areas in Massachusetts, thus alleviating the pressure on well known and heavily used mountain biking spots around Greater Boston.

Soft Cycling

Because of the perception that mountain bikes are unsafe and environmentally damaging, many states across the country have closed trails to off-road cycling. Most notably, California has closed all state forest and park trails to mountain bikes, except for trails specifically posted as open. Other states are following suit and more closures are likely to occur. Fortunately, Massachusetts has seen no such broad-based limitations on mountain bike trail access, at least not yet. While mountain bikes are restricted in certain state forests, parks and public reservations, most land management organizations in Massachusetts have taken a careful approach in defining policies for the use of mountain bikes, studying the current impact of bikes on the trails and gathering input from various trail user groups. The next few years will be crucial in determining the future of trail access for mountain bikes in Massachusetts. If mountain bikers can prove themselves capable of safely and responsibly sharing the trails, more land will remain unrestricted; if the perception of mountain bikes as "two-wheeled terrors" continues to grow, many trails will likely be closed. The actions of each and every rider contribute to the public's perception of the sport of mountain biking. It is up to you to learn to ride safely and responsibly at all times. Riding responsibly can be frustrating—it's no fun to have to slow down constantly to pass hikers on long descents, to stop and walk around a section of muddy trail that you could easily ride, or to skip a ride on your favorite trail because it's still wet from a recent rain. But each hiker you scare by passing too quickly, each equestrian you force off the trail and each rut you dig will increase the chances that the trail you are riding on today will be closed to you tomorrow. The compromises of responsible riding are a small price to pay for continued trail access.

The International Mountain Bicycling Association, an organization which promotes open trails through responsible and environmentally sound cycling, has prepared a general set of trail rules that have become the responsible mountain biker's creed. Be familiar with these rules and obey them at all times.

IMBA Rules of the Trail

1. Ride on open trails only. Respect trail and road closures (ask if not sure), avoid possible trespass on private land, obtain permits and

authorization as may be required. Federal and state wilderness areas are closed to cycling.

2. Leave no trace. Be sensitive to the dirt beneath you. Even on open trails, you should not ride under conditions where you will leave evidence of your passing, such as on certain soils shortly after a rain. Observe the different types of soils and trail construction; practice low-impact cycling. This also means staying on the trail and not creating any new ones. Be sure to pack out at least as much as you pack in.

3. Control your bicycle! Inattention for even a second can cause disaster. Excessive speed maims and threatens people; there is no excuse for it!

4. Always yield the trail. Make known your approach well in advance. A friendly greeting (or bell) is considerate and works well; startling someone may cause loss of trail access. Show your respect when passing others by slowing to a walk or even stopping. Anticipate that other trail users may be around corners or in blind spots.

5. Never spook animals. All animals are startled by an unannounced approach, a sudden movement or a loud noise. This can be dangerous for you, for others and for the animals. Give animals extra room and time to adjust to you. In passing, use special care and follow the directions of horseback riders (ask if uncertain). Running cattle and disturbing wild animals is a serious offense. Leave gates as you found them, or as marked.

6. Plan ahead. Know your equipment, your ability and the area in which you are riding—and prepare accordingly. Be self-sufficient at all times. Wear a helmet, keep your machine in good condition, and carry necessary supplies for changes in weather or other conditions. A well executed trip is a satisfaction to you and not a burden or offense to others.

(IMBA Rules of the Trial, ©1990, International Mountain Bicycling Association)

In addition, the following guidelines emphasize particular aspects of the IMBA rules:

• Yield the trail to hikers. When overtaking a hiker, slow down to a near-walking pace and move to the side of the trail; don't make the hiker move off the trail for you. Even if the trail is wide enough to pass safely at high speed, please don't—you may know that you are completely in control of your bike, but the person you are zooming by won't. Also, don't sneak up on people—even if you are moving slowly, you will startle someone who doesn't know you are coming.

- Yield the trail to equestrians. If you scare a horse it may bolt or kick out, harming its rider, itself or you. When approaching a horse from the front, stop and move well off the trail until it passes. When approaching from behind, call ahead to the rider from a safe distance to make sure it's okay to pass.

- Avoid riding on muddy trails. Do not ride on trails during or just after a rain, or during the mud season. If you encounter sections of muddy trail, dismount and walk around them. Riding through mud puddles creates ruts and causes erosion. Riding around them is even worse, as it creates "blow-outs," widened sections of rutted trail. Also be careful when crossing streams, water bars or other wet areas that are easily susceptible to damage.

- Don't skid. Control your speed and apply your brakes smoothly. Ride slowly when ascending or descending steep sections of trail, especially on loose dirt, to prevent tearing up the trail.

- Ride or walk *over* obstacles on the trail. Never ride around them, as this damages vegetation and creates new, unwanted trails.

- Always wear a helmet.

- Always ride with another person. Leave word with someone as to where you are planning to go and when you plan to return.

- Be aware of hunting activity. At 200 yards, it's easy to mistake the distant blur of a rider whizzing down the trail for a buck bounding through the woods. If hunting activity is high, wear bright-colored clothing.

Selecting a Ride

Each chapter in this book gives directions, a map and historical background for an off-road mountain bike ride. The rides vary greatly in distance, difficulty and type of terrain covered. Selecting a ride that meets your interests and level of ability will enhance your enjoyment. The distance, difficulty and type of terrain for each tour is listed at the beginning of each chapter. Use this information as well as the introductory paragraphs of each chapter to choose an appropriate ride.

Difficulty and Distance.   The difficulty of each tour is rated from Easy to Difficult, based on the types of trails covered and the steepness of the terrain. Trail type ranges from wide, smooth dirt roads to narrow, rocky foot trails. The steepness of the terrain ranges from flat to mountainous. The difficulty rating of a tour is a combination of these two factors: a flat ride on wide dirt roads is rated Easy; a rolling ride on dirt paths, Moderate; and a hilly ride on narrow trails, Difficult. These ratings must be considered relative to your own experience and ability as a mountain biker. A first-time rider may find all but the easiest rides in this book daunting, while an experienced racer will be able to ride them all without much trouble. It is also important to remember that the difficulty rating is assigned independently of a ride's distance. An 18-mile ride rated Easy is still 18 miles of biking. Even if the trails are completely flat it will be a challenging tour if you are not used to riding such a distance off-road.

Terrain.   On almost every tour described in this book, the terrain can vary greatly along the course of the ride. The ratings represent the average difficulty of each tour, but even the easy tours will have some difficult sections, and the difficult tours will have some easy ones. If you encounter a part of the trail that is more than you can handle, dismount and walk until you reach an easier section. Don't expect to be able to ride the entire trail, especially the first time out. Walking or carrying your bike is part of mountain biking, and even the best riders encounter hills too steep to ride or logs too big to jump. As your riding skills improve, you will find yourself riding more and walking less.

Riding Speed.   The speed at which you can expect to ride these tours will vary with your ability, the difficulty of the trail, your familiarity with the route and the attitude with which you approach the ride. The same trail that took all day to ride when you packed a picnic lunch and set out with a group of friends for a relaxed tour in the country can be ridden in two hours on another day when you approach it as a high-speed, non-stop training ride. Route finding is time consuming, and it takes much longer to ride trails you are not familiar with than ones you have ridden before. As a rough guideline, figure on averaging four to five miles per hour on tours you are riding for the first time, and eight to ten miles per hour once you are familiar with a route. When planning a ride, always allow extra time for rest stops, route finding and unexpected breakdowns.

Other Trails.   Most of the rides given in this book are on trails located within a particular recreation area, such as a state forest, park or public reservation. Often, the route described in each chapter is just one possible ride in an area that has many different trails. Many of the tours are designed to give an overview of a trail system, so that once you have ridden the route described in the chapter you can go back and find more trails on your own. Don't let the distance or difficulty rating of a tour keep you from visiting a particular riding area as you will almost always be able to lengthen or shorten a ride, and find trails that are easier or harder than the ones covered in the chapter.

Route Finding

Before you set out, it's important to understand that following a tour for the first time will require a significant amount of effort. Most places to ride in Massachusetts have a maze of interconnected trails, many of which are not marked and do not appear on any map, and this makes route finding problematic. The map and written directions in each chapter are designed to help you find your way through these mazes, but they will only be useful if you pay close attention to them. This can mean stopping frequently to figure out where you are and where you should be going next. Doing so can be slow and frustrating, breaking up the pace of a ride, but it is necessary to keep from getting lost. If you ride without heeding landmarks, it's easy to miss a turn or pass by a fork without realizing it. Following are some tips that will make route finding easier:

- The directions given are designed to take maximum advantage of landmarks, intersections, trail markers, blazes and other features of the landscape. They usually begin with such designations as, At a fork, As you reach a pond on the left, As the trail turns sharply right, At a double blue blaze, etc. Always read one direction ahead of your current position so you will know what landmark to look for next.

- The directions specify every turn you must take to follow a route, but they don't point out each and every trail you will pass along the way. Always assume that if the directions do not tell you to turn onto a particular trail, you should continue straight on the trail you are on. If you reach a fork or a T intersection where a decision is necessary, the directions will tell you which way to turn.

- Each time you turn onto a new trail the directions give its name, if it has one. If the trail is marked by a sign then the name is included in the text of the direction. If there is no sign, the trail name is placed in parentheses at the end of the direction.

- An odometer is not essential, but it will make following the directions much easier. If you don't have an odometer, it's still crucial to pay attention to the mileage figures given for each direction so you will know whether the next landmark is a tenth of a mile or a mile and a half down the trail.

- If you photocopy the directions before you set out and carry them in a convenient place, you won't have to pull out the entire book to find the right page every time you stop.

- Always be sure to pick up the recommended maps listed at the beginning of each chapter. The maps given in this book show the route of a ride as accurately as possible in the space available, but there may be times when you will need the greater detail only a full-sized map can provide.

Maps

Both the bane and the salvation of mountain bikers trying to find their way around the convoluted trail systems of Massachusetts, a map is essential if want to do anything more ambitious than wander around aimlessly for an afternoon. Unfortunately, many of the maps available for mountain biking are at best incomplete and at worst inaccurate. Still, you are better off with a map than without one.

The most common limitations of maps are that they do not show enough detail, or they are outdated, with roads and trails changed, added or dropped since the map was made. Maps almost never show every trail you will encounter, and sometimes even show trails that no longer exist! For example, what looks like the first right turn off the road you are on can actually be the third right turn because the map does not show the two intervening dirt roads that have been constructed since the map was made. Or, there may be a fork on the trail where no fork is shown on the map because one of the trails off the fork was too small to be included on the map. Because trails and roads change so frequently, it is therefore best to navigate by using more stable landmarks whenever possible. Stream crossings, power lines, hills, cliffs, swamps and other natural or man-made features *are* usually marked on maps and offer invaluable clues. If you know that the next right turn is just after a stream and under a set of power lines you should have no trouble finding it, even if the map does not indicate every trail you might pass in getting there.

Before setting out for a ride, pick up the recommended maps listed at the beginning of each chapter. They are listed in order of usefulness, but it is often helpful to get all the maps available for a particular area as each will show a different subset of actual trails, giving you a more complete picture of the trail system. When two maps of the same type are listed for a ride, such as two USGS maps or two state forest maps, you need both to cover the entire area of the tour.

The maps in this book have been drawn based on data from one of the three types of maps described below, and therefore may share some of their inaccuracies. Wherever possible, problems have been corrected and missing trails added.

State Forest, Park and Reservation Maps.   These are usually free of charge at forest, park or reservation headquarters. They vary greatly in quality, depending on how old they are and how much care went into making them. Most are not very detailed, and the trails and roads shown on them are rough approximations of the actual terrain. Many are printed according to a standard format but have a confusing and sometimes inconsistent key, with hiking trails, bridle paths, skiing trails, hiking/skiing and hiking/bridle paths designated by different markings.

United States Geological Survey (USGS) Maps.   The USGS puts out two series of topographical maps that between them cover every part of Massachusetts. Despite their official look, these maps are not necessarily more complete or accurate than any other map for mountain biking purposes, as they are often drawn to a level of detail that does not include foot trails and are sometimes out of date. The USGS maps will usually show all the paved roads, most of the dirt roads, some of the dirt paths and only a few of the foot trails in an area. The level of detail varies from map to map, so some will be better about showing foot trails and dirt paths than others. These maps can range from extremely helpful to completely useless for mountain biking, depending on whether or not the map of a particular area shows the trails you want to ride. But they are worth taking along even if they don't show every trail because they provide helpful information about terrain. However, you should look closely at a USGS map before buying it to make sure it shows at least some of the trails you intend to ride. The map list at the beginning of each chapter generally gives the USGS map for the tour if it provides any useful information. Usually, but not always, if there is a map of the specific state forest, park or reservation, it will be more useful than the USGS map of the same area.

The USGS maps for Massachusetts come in two formats. The older 7.5′ maps are in a square, flat format, with a scale of 1:24,000 and distances in feet and miles. These are being replaced by folded rect-angular 7.5′ × 15′ maps, with a scale of 1:25,000 and distances in meters. The newer 7.5′ × 15′ maps are preferable since they show twice the area of the 7.5′ maps, tend to be more up-to-date and are easier to carry. However, the 7.5′ × 15′ maps are not yet available for all areas, and they sometimes omit hiking trails that were shown on the older 7.5′ maps; so using the older 7.5′ maps is sometimes necessary.

New England Cartographics (NEC) Maps. NEC produces topo-graphic maps for numerous popular hiking areas in central and western Massachusetts. These are sold at many outdoor stores around the state and are by far the most detailed, accurate and complete of any available. If a NEC map is listed for a particular ride, by all means use it. Although the level of detail shown on these maps can make them confusing at first, once you get used to reading them they are very helpful.

Sources for Maps

USGS maps can be difficult to find, so you might have to visit several places to get the one you need. They are often sold in sporting goods stores that carry hiking equipment and can also be found in some bookstores. Many stores carry a partial and changing selection as the maps are popular and the USGS is notorious for slow and inaccurate filling of orders.

Below is a listing of some Boston area stores that have a good selection of USGS maps and libraries with a complete collection that you can photocopy, as well as the address of the USGS, from which you may order maps directly.

Hammett's, 147 Friend Street, Boston (617-523-5778)

Harvard Square Map Store, 49 Palmer Street, Cambridge (617-497-6277)

R.E.I., 279 Salem Street (exit 40 off MA 128), Reading (617-944-5103)

Lincoln Guide Service, 152 Lincoln Road, Lincoln (617-259-9204)

Wilderness House, 1048 Commonwealth Avenue, Boston (617-277-5858)

Massachusetts Institute of Technology, Science Library Map Room, 160 Memorial Drive, Cambridge (617-253-5685)

Boston Public Library, 666 Boylston Street, Boston (617-536-5400)

New England Cartographics, P.O. Box 369, Amherst, MA 01004 (413-253-7415)

United States Geological Survey, Map Sales, Box 25286, Denver, CO 80225 (303-236-7477)

Selecting a Mountain Bike

To ride the tours in this book you will need a bike designed for off-road riding. The features of an off-road bike include:

- Flat handlebars

- Low-rise handlebar stem

- 26″ wheels

- Wide, knobby tires

- Extra-strong frame

- 18 or 21 gears, with low gears for hill climbing

It is worth investing in a good bike if you plan to ride frequently. Off-road riding is very punishing to a bike, and if yours isn't built to withstand the stresses of riding on rough trails you'll eventually find yourself stranded in the woods with a long walk ahead of you. It's always best to get a bike made by a reputable manufacturer from a store specializing in bicycles or sports equipment, even if you can only afford an entry-level model. While you could save a few dollars by buying a department store bike, chances are it won't hold up for long. But a quality bike, if properly maintained, can last indefinitely. If you think of your bike as being a ten- or twenty-year investment, it makes sense to pay a little more now for one that will last. Today, well-made mountain bikes start as low as $275-$325. Many in this entry-level price range are city/off-road bikes, meaning that they have higher gears and narrower tires than a strictly off-road bike, and raised handlebars that allow you a more upright position. Such bikes are easily modified for off-road riding by adding a pair of wide, knobby tires and a set of toe clips and straps.

As the price goes up from the entry-level models, bikes tend to be better designed for off-road riding, with wider tires, lower gears and flat handlebars and stems. In each successively higher priced category, the bikes are stronger and lighter, with better quality, smoother and more responsive components. The differences between each price category are small but significant, and the improvements add up—the feel of a $600 bike will be noticeably different from that of a $300 bike.

Fit is as important in making a selection as the quality of a bike's components. Choose one small enough so you have at least three or four inches of clearance when standing over the top tube, but large enough so you can raise the saddle sufficiently high to allow you to fully extend your legs when riding. There's no advantage in getting a bike bigger than necessary as a larger frame adds more weight. Many mountain bikes have extra long seatposts that let you choose a small frame but still allow you to raise the seat to a road-riding height. It is also important to find a bike with the proper top-tube length—the length of the bike from saddle to handlebars. There is no hard and fast rule for determining ideal top-tube length; you want a bike that makes you feel neither too stretched nor too cramped when you ride. The only way to find the right top-tube fit is to try several bikes and choose the one that feels most comfortable.

Nearly every major manufacturer offers a selection of quality off-road bikes, and within a particular price range the differences between brands are very small; you may find three or four bikes for the same price, with the same basic components, that fit equally well. The choice often amounts to small details such as the type of saddle, pedals or handlebar grips used. For more detailed information on selecting a bicycle and accessories, consult a book such as Norman D. Ford's *Keep On Pedaling: The Complete Guide to Adult Bicycling* (The Countryman Press, Woodstock, VT, 1990).

Keep in mind that the most important thing is never to let your equipment hold you back on the trails. You can have fun off-road on just about anything with two wheels and a chain. The first mountain bikers in California during the late 1970's proved this point well. Their bikes were 60-pound, one-speed clunkers, yet they rode trails that were more difficult than any described in this book and still managed to have enough fun so as to introduce a whole new sport.

Additional Bike Equipment, Accessories and Modifications

In addition to a good off-road bike, there are a number of accessories you may want to purchase to enhance the safety, comfort and off-road performance of your rides. Among the most important of these are the following:

Toe Clips and Straps.   Toe clips and straps are essential for off-road riding, giving you more control over the bike and keeping your feet from slipping off the pedals on rough descents. As long as the straps are loose they do not hinder you from taking a foot off the pedal to stop, and you can always use the bottom of the pedal if you need to keep a foot free while riding a particularly difficult section of trail.

Toe Flips. Toe flips are small metal or plastic tabs that can be bolted onto the front of the pedal to let your shoes easily grab the pedal and flip it around. They make getting into your toe clips immeasurably easier, especially when starting from a stop on an uphill. Some pedals have small toe flips built in, but if yours do not, Wilderness Trail Bikes makes a well designed set that attaches to almost any pedal.

Water-Bottle Cages. Two frame-mounted water-bottle cages will allow you to carry plenty of easily accessible water.

Reflectors. Almost all new bikes come equipped with reflectors and almost all new bike owners remove them as soon as they get home. If you take the reflectors off your bike, sooner or later you'll find yourself riding home at dusk wishing you'd left them on. As an alternative to standard reflectors, consider Sidelights, adhesive-backed reflective strips that attach to your rims and which are highly visible to passing motorists.

Odometer. Though not absolutely necessary, an odometer makes it easier to follow the directions given for each tour.

Tires. A pair of aggressive off-road tires is the best way to improve a bike's performance on the trails. Wide, knobby tires increase your bike's traction and help absorb the shock of rough trails. Use the widest tires that will fit your bike, and keep them inflated at 35-45 psi for optimum performance off-road.

Gearing. The lower the gears, the easier it is to ascend steep hills and maintain a steady pace on long climbs. Many bikes do not come with low enough gears for hilly off-road riding, but most can be modified easily by adding a smaller chainring in front or a larger freewheel cog in back.

Underseat Bag. A small bag attached under your saddle provides a convenient place to carry a patch kit, tire repair levers, spare tube and other essential tools you will want to have on your bike at all times.

Rider Accessories

Helmet. Falls occur more frequently from mountain bikes than from road bikes, and hitting rocks or trees can cause serious head injuries. The newest bike helmets are cool, light and comfortable, eliminating any reason ever to ride without one.

Clothing. Padded bike shorts make long hours on a bike seat more comfortable. Uncleated bike shoes designed for touring or specifically for mountain biking have stiff insoles and shallow cleats that make pedaling more efficient than ordinary sneakers. In cool weather, dress-

ing in layered clothing lets you adjust your body temperature to stay warm and dry. A wicking bottom layer will let perspiration evaporate, and a water-resistant top layer will keep out rain, spray and mud.

Gloves. Padded gloves ease shock and pressure on your hands. Gloves made specifically for mountain biking, with ¾-length fingers and gel-padded palms, provide an extra measure of comfort.

Food and Water. In warmer weather, carrying two large (20 ounce) water-bottles is mandatory for all but the shortest rides in this book. If you only have a single water-bottle cage, carry a second leak-proof bottle in your pack. Bring some high energy food along as well to keep you nourished on longer rides.

Insect Repellent. A small bottle of the strongest insect repellent available is essential for protection from mosquitoes and other biting flies during the spring and summer.

Fanny Pack. Most riders prefer a fanny pack for carrying the gear needed for a day on the trails. Use one to hold food, extra water, a rain jacket or warm shirt, maps and, of course, a copy of this book.

Riding Technique

Anyone who knows how to ride a bicycle can hop on a mountain bike and hit the trails, but the more you ride off-road the more you realize that mountain biking is a very different sport from road biking, with an entirely new set of skills and techniques to be learned. Below is a brief description of a few essential techniques with which every rider should be familiar before venturing off-road.

Handlebar Grip.   Use a two-finger grip when riding on flat ground and down hills: your index and middle fingers of each hand hold the brake lever while your other two fingers and thumb grip the handlebars. This grip allows you to brake and steer the bike simultaneously.

Descent Position.   When going downhill, stand up on the pedals and shift your weight toward the back of the bike. Keep the pedal cranks horizontal to the ground and grip the saddle between your thighs. The steeper the descent, the farther back your weight should be on the bike. It may help to lower your saddle on steep descents.

Clearing Obstacles.   Most moderate-sized logs can be ridden over easily by lifting your front tire. Approach at a comfortable rate of speed; just before reaching the log, pedal hard and pull the handlebars sharply back and up to lift the front wheel up and over the log. After your front wheel is over, shift your weight forward to allow your back wheel to roll over the log. Use caution on logs that are wet or lying at an angle to the trail.

Tools

Mountain bikes are marvels of engineering that can withstand almost anything. Still, they do break down occasionally, and the inconvenience can be considerable, especially if you're miles away from help. So it's worth the extra weight to carry a few essential tools when you ride. At minimum, you should be able to fix a flat tire. Although the wide tires of mountain bikes are relatively impervious to flats, they do occur, especially when riding through thorns. To fix a flat, you will need:

Tire Levers.   Two nylon tire levers to remove the tire from the rim.

Patch Kit.   These generally include patches, cement and a piece of sandpaper to rough up the tube. A small piece of chalk to mark the site of the leak is also handy.

Pump.   Any pump that fits the valves on your wheels will do, though the pumps made specifically for mountain biking are stronger than those made for road biking; strap it to your bike to keep it from bouncing off on bumpy trails, and use a small plastic plug to keep mud out of the valve opening.

Spare Tube. Although you can get by without a spare tube if you have a patch kit, a tube will make tire repairs quicker and will save you from walking if your tire has a broken valve stem that can't be patched.

To be prepared to fix more extensive problems than a flat tire, you should carry the following items:

Chain Tool Rivet Extractor. Chains and derailleurs are the most vulnerable parts of a mountain bike. If you break a link on your chain, a chain tool will allow you to remove the broken link and repair the chain. If you break your rear derailleur, it will allow you to shorten the chain around a single chainring and cog, bypassing the derailleur. This will turn your bike into a one-speed, but it's a better alternative than a long walk home.

Spare Chain Links. Four or five extra links can be used to repair a broken chain.

Allen Wrenches. Carry one for tightening every size bolt on your bike.

Small Adjustable Wrench. Use for adjusting brakes and tightening bolts.

Spoke Wrench. Use to straighten a severely bent wheel or replace a broken spoke.

Screwdrivers. Carry both a small Phillips head and a flat blade screwdriver for adjusting derailleurs and tightening loose screws.

Spray Lubricant. Take a small bottle for lubricating the chain and other moving parts.

Tire boot. A 3″ × 3″ piece of rubber cut from an old tire can be used to cover a hole in a tire by placing it over the hole on the tire's inside; once the tube is inflated, the pressure of the tube against the tire will hold the boot in place.

Assorted Nuts and Bolts. Use for repairing broken pedals, racks, etc.

Duct Tape. Wrap some around a tire lever or wrench handle; it comes in handy for all kinds of emergency repairs.

Cool Tool. This is a single tool that combines an adjustable wrench, 4-, 5- and 6-mm Allen wrenches, a Phillips head screwdriver and a crank bolt tool in one compact, lightweight unit; you can carry a Cool Tool instead of many of the above-mentioned tools (available from Cool Tool, 13524 Autumn Lane, Chico, CA 95926, 916-893-3079).

For longer trips, you may also wish to include the following tools and parts in your repair kit:

Cone Wrenches. Use for adjusting loose wheel hubs.

Spare Cables. Carry one brake and one derailleur cable to replace broken ones.

Small Cable Cutters. Use for installing new cables.

Spare Spokes. Use to replace broken ones.

Freewheel Removal Tool. Use to remove a freewheel in order to repair broken spokes on the freewheel side of the rear wheel. For older bikes, you also need a large wrench, vise, or pocket vise to remove the freewheel; for newer bikes with cassette-style freehubs, Pamir makes a small, lightweight freewheel removal tool that is perfect for trailside repairs (available from Pamir Engineering, P.O. Box 942, Boylston, MA 01505).

Headset Wrench. Use for tightening a loose headset.

Maintenance
A little bit of maintenance goes a long way on a mountain bike. Dirt and mud are damaging to a bicycle's moving parts, so it is essential to keep your bike clean and well lubricated. After riding in wet or muddy conditions, wash off your bike thoroughly with a hose, wipe it down with a dry cloth and lubricate the chain with a spray lubricant such as Tri-flow. Mountain bike brakes need to be adjusted frequently to compensate for brake-pad wear. This is easily done by turning the knobs on the brake levers to shorten the brake cable. Small adjustments to the rear derailleur are also easy to make, usually requiring just a turn or two of the knob on the rear shifter to tighten or loosen the derailleur cable. Bringing your bike to a reputable shop for a tune-up every six months to a year will keep it running smoothly and minimize the chance of a breakdown on the trail.

Sources of Information About Mountain Biking

Mountain Bike Organizations
    National Off-Road Bicycle Association, 1750 East Boulder Street, Colorado Springs, CO 80909 (719-578-4717). The National Off-Road Bicycle Association (NORBA) serves as the governing association for mountain bike racing. NORBA sanctions many off-road races and provides race officials, scheduling assistance and materials to organizations that promote mountain bike races. You must be a NORBA member to race in many mountain bike races.
    International Mountain Bicycling Association, Route 2, Box 303, Bishop, CA 93514 (619-387-2757). The International Mountain Bicycling Association (IMBA) is a volunteer nonprofit organization whose goal is to keep public lands open for recreational enjoyment by responsible moun-

tain bikers. Toward that goal they publish a newsletter, *Land Access Alert,* as a means of keeping members informed of current issues and events. They also promote educational efforts that benefit cyclists and the public at large, educating cyclists on the safe, courteous and environmentally sound use of mountain bikes, and informing the public of the low impact of mountain cycling and cyclists' willingness to cooperate with other trail users.

New England Mountain Bicycling Association, 69 Spring Street, Cambridge, MA 02141. (617-497-6891) The New England Mountain Bicycling Association (NEMBA) is a regional affiliate of IMBA and represents the interests of mountain bicyclists in New England. NEMBA acts as a liaison between reservation landowners and mountain bicyclists to promote awareness of the possible environmental impact of mountain biking. They also work with land management organizations to coordinate trail maintenance and cleanup efforts, and to represent mountain bikers in the formation of trail use policies. If you ride a mountain bike in New England, you should join NEMBA.

Bicycle Institute of America, 1878 R. Street NW, Washington, DC 20009 (202-332-6986). The Bicycle Institute of America (BIA) works with IMBA to promote the sport of mountain biking and continued trail access for mountain bikes. BIA distributes a *Bike Hiking Action Kit* that includes information on trail access, sample letters to send to public officials and newspapers, and suggestions on how to increase public understanding of mountain bike trail access issues.

League of American Wheelmen, 6707 Whitestone Road, Suite 209, Baltimore, MD 21207 (301-944-3399). The League of American Wheelmen (LAW) works with IMBA and BIA to promote the sports of bicycling and mountain biking.

Bikecentennial, P.O. Box 8308, Missoula, MT 59807 (406-721-1776). Bikecentennial is a bicycle travel association that provides maps, guidebooks and information on road and mountain bike touring.

Mountain Bike Tours and Schools

Velotours, 49 Front Street, Marblehead, MA 01945 (617-631-6184). Velotours runs on- and off-road bicycle tours in Massachusetts and throughout New England, including mountain bike tours of the Cape Ann (Gloucester and Rockport) area.

Mt. Snow Mountain Bike School, Mt. Snow Ski Resort, Mt. Snow, VT 03356 (802-464-3333 x328). The Mt. Snow Mountain Bike School offers two- to three-day classes on mountain biking skills and techniques. The classes are appropriate for riders of all levels of ability, and offer a mix of individualized and group instruction and trail riding. The classes are given weekends from Memorial Day until the weekend following Columbus Day.

Land Management Organizations

Massachusetts Department of Environmental Management, Division of Forests and Parks, 100 Cambridge Street, Boston, MA 02202 (617-727-3180). The Division of Forests and Parks manages over 250,000 acres of state forest, park and reservation land in Massachusetts. The Division publishes a guide to Massachusetts forests and parks that is available free of charge at many state forest headquarters.

The Trustees of Reservations, 572 Essex Street, Beverly, MA 01915 (508-921-1944). The Trustees of Reservations is an organization dedicated to protecting the natural landscape by acquisition of open land. They are the largest private owner of conservation land in Massachusetts, owning 70 properties that total almost 18,000 acres, including beach areas, wildlife refuges and historic houses. Their properties are open for hiking, nature study, canoeing and other activities, usually for a small fee. Mountain biking is allowed at some, but not all, of the Trustees of Reservations properties.

Metropolitan District Commission, 20 Somerset Street, Boston, MA 02202 (617-727-5215). The Metropolitan District Commission, through its MetroParks service, manages parkland and reservations around the Greater Boston area.

Magazines

Bicycling Plus Mountain Bike, 33 East Minor Street, Emmaus, PA 18098 (215-967-5171).

Mountain and City Biking, 7950 Deering Avenue, Canoga Park, CA 91304 (818-887-0550).

Mountain Bike Action, 10600 Sepulveda Boulevard, Mission Hills, CA 91345 (818-365-6831).

Bicycle Guide, 711 Boylston Street, Boston, MA 02116 (617-236-1885).

Fat Tire Flyer, P.O. Box 757, Fairfax, CA 94930 (415-457-7016).

Books

Bicycling Magazine's Mountain Biking Skills, Rodale Press, 1990.

Dennis Coello, *The Complete Mountain Biker,* Lyons and Burford, 1989.

Dennis Coello, *The Mountain Bike Repair Handbook,* Lyons and Burford, 1990.

Norman D. Ford, *Keep on Pedaling: The Complete Guide to Adult Bicycling,* The Countryman Press, 1990.

Summary of Tours

The following is a summary of tours arranged by difficulty and distance within each region.

No.	Location	Difficulty	Distance (miles)
	GREATER BOSTON		
2.	Middlesex Fells	Easy to moderate	8.0
1.	Lynn Woods	Easy to moderate	9.0
	NORTH OF BOSTON		
6.	Great Brook Farm State Park	Easy	5.0
8.	Plum Island	Easy	21.6
9.	Ravenswood Park	Easy to moderate	4.8
7.	Harold Parker State Forest	Easy to moderate	9.6
5.	Dogtown	Moderate	10.8
4.	Bradley Palmer State Park and Willowdale State Forest	Moderate	17.2
	SOUTH OF BOSTON		
14.	Martha's Vineyard	Easy	6.0
16.	Rocky Woods	Easy to moderate	2.7/4.9
15.	Nickerson State Park	Easy to moderate	7.4
10.	Borderland State Park	Easy to moderate	7.7
17.	Wompatuck State Park	Easy to moderate	8.2
12.	Freetown - Fall River State Forest	Easy to moderate	10.9
13.	Hale Reservation	Moderate	9.7
11.	F. Gilbert Hills State Forest	Moderate to difficult	8.2
	CENTRAL MASSACHUSETTS		
21.	Ware River Watershed	Easy to moderate	16.4
18.	Harvard Forest	Moderate	15.1
20.	Wachusett Mountain	Moderate to difficult	11.8
19.	Otter River State Forest	Moderate to difficult	18.5
	CONNECTICUT RIVER VALLEY		
23.	Metacomet-Monadnock Trail	Moderate	9.3/18.6
25.	Northfield Mountain	Moderate to difficult	9.3
24.	Mount Toby	Difficult	12.2
22.	Holyoke Range State Park	Difficult	18.2

Lynn Woods

Distance: 9.0 miles
Terrain: Rolling dirt road and forest trail
Difficulty: Easy to moderate
Map: Lynn Woods (available at Lynn City Hall); USGS 7.5′ × 15′ Lynn

Who would know that Lynn, the grimy industrial city north of Boston, has trapped within its confines one of the largest municipal parks in the country? Lynn is a city known more for its shoe manufacturing than for its great outdoor spaces. It's a pleasant surprise, then, to discover Lynn Woods—2,200 acres of rocky forest only ten miles from downtown Boston. The roads, trails and bridle paths that cross Lynn Woods offer a gamut of riding possibilities, as well as a chance to explore the caves and crags of an area steeped in the legends of Lynn's colonial past.

Since Lynn was first settled in 1629, Lynn Woods has been set aside as a place unto itself. Too rocky to farm, and too hilly to build on, the woods provided no value to the colonists except as a place for their animals to graze and as a convenient source of firewood. The early settlers built stone walls dividing the woods into three sections, each named according to its use: the land closest to town was the cow pasture, the middle tract the horse pasture, and the farthest reaches the ox pasture. The land was held in common by the citizens of Lynn until, tradition has it, the settlers heard rumors of a boatload of new colonists on their way from the mother country. They quickly divided the common land into individually held lots so that its wealth would not be diluted by the arrival of the newcomers. Many of the tracts comprising Lynn Woods remained within the families of their original owners until 1899, when the city raised $45,000 to purchase the land for use as a park.

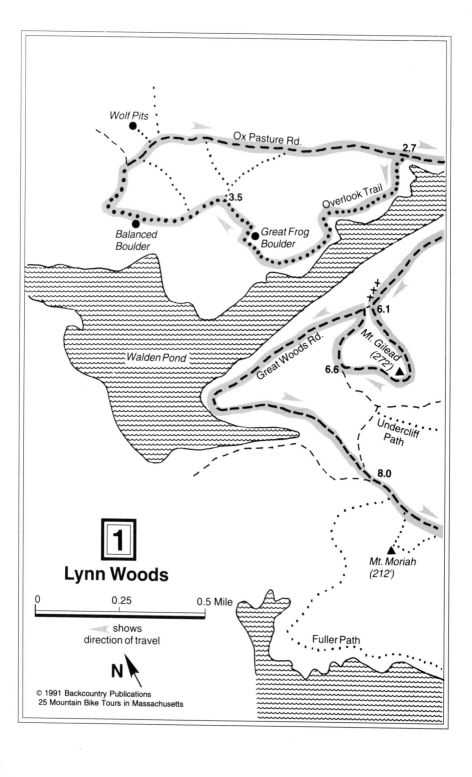

Wolf Pits

Ox Pasture Rd.

2.7

3.5

Overlook Trail

Great Frog Boulder

Balanced Boulder

6.1

Mt. Gilead *(272')*

Great Woods Rd.

6.6

Walden Pond

Undercliff Path

8.0

1

Lynn Woods

Mt. Moriah *(212')*

0   0.25   0.5 Mile

◄ shows
direction of travel

N

Fuller Path

© 1991 Backcountry Publications
25 Mountain Bike Tours in Massachusetts

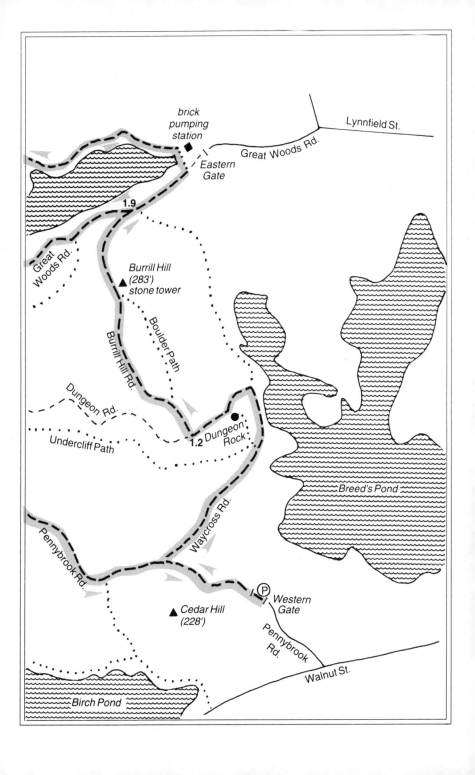

Since its creation as a park, Lynn Woods has had its ups and downs. In its heyday, visitors flocked there to hike its craggy trails, picnic in its lush forests and view the sweeping coastline from its observation towers. Unfortunately, funding cutbacks in recent years have made it impossible for the City of Lynn to maintain the land. The observation towers are closed, and in some places the trails are littered with broken glass and rusted metal and cluttered by abandoned cars. Despite these drawbacks, the park is still an enjoyable place to ride and is one of only a few large tracts of open land in the metropolitan Boston area. Although surrounded by city, sections of the park can be surprisingly remote, taking you far away from the urban rush.

This ride completes a wide circuit of Lynn Woods, staying mainly on the network of dirt roads that run through the park. These dirt roads are easy to ride and follow, and give a good overview of the park's terrain, going by many of its ponds, hills and historical sites. If you are looking for a more challenging ride, the park is also crisscrossed by narrower, rockier bridle paths and hiking trails.

To Get There: From MA 128 (I-95) take exit 44A for US 1 South, Everett, Boston. Follow US 1 South for 2.1 miles to the exit for Walnut Street, Lynn. At the end of the exit ramp turn right onto Walnut Street. Follow Walnut Street for 2.1 miles, then turn left at a traffic signal onto Pennybrook Road. In 0.3 mile, pass through a stone gate (Western Gate) into Lynn Woods. Park in the dirt lot immediately on the right after going through the gate.

The Ride

0.0 The ride begins at Lynn Woods' western gate. Start on the paved road that runs from the gate into the park (Pennybrook Road). After 100 yards, go through a black and red metal gate and continue STRAIGHT on a wide dirt road.

0.3 Turn RIGHT onto a dirt road (Waycross Road).

As you ride along this road you pass Breed's Pond, built by Theophilus N. Breed in 1843 to power a nearby ironworks. The pond was purchased as an emergency water supply by the City of Lynn after a devastating fire in 1869.

1.0 As you reach the top of a hill, a gravel path lined with stones on both sides leads to the left toward Dungeon Rock.

An imposing cliff split down the middle by a deep crevice, Dungeon Rock has spawned a curious legend of pirates and treasure hunters. The story begins on a summer night in 1656, when a mysterious, unmarked ship was seen sailing into Lynn and anchoring off the coast. The ship attracted the attention of the people of Lynn, and later that night four men were seen being dropped from the ship in a

small boat and rowing up the Saugus River. The next day the mystery ship was gone, leaving only one clue as to the purpose of its visit: a message found at the nearby Saugus Ironworks stating that if a quantity of iron shackles, handcuffs and other articles were left at a certain spot in the woods, they would be paid for in silver.

The requested items were made and deposited at the designated spot. Some time later they disappeared and a pile of silver was found in their place. Although the harbor was watched closely, the mystery ship was never seen again and no one knew who collected the items or how they had been spirited away. The story of these strange events spread swiftly around town, and rumor had it that it was the work of pirates.

A few months later, four men snuck into Lynn Woods and secluded themselves in a remote, narrow valley where they built a hut, planted a garden and dug a well. It was presumed that they were the very same men who had been seen rowing up the Saugus River. Although they were well hidden, eventually word of their presence spread to the authorities. They were suspected of being pirates, and the King's soldiers came to arrest them. One, Thomas Veal, escaped and hid in a cave at Dungeon Rock. He lived there for a few years, working occasionally as a shoemaker and visiting town to buy supplies. In 1658, an earthquake struck, collapsing Veal's home and burying him in a dungeon of rock. The people of Lynn suspected that the four pirates had brought treasure with them to Lynn Woods, but since nothing was ever found it was supposed that the treasure, along with Veal, was sealed forever inside Dungeon Rock.

The rock rested undisturbed for almost 200 years until 1852, when the property around Dungeon Rock was purchased by a man named Hiram Marble. A devout spiritualist, Marble had been told by a medium that he would find buried treasure somewhere along the north shore of Boston, and he chose Dungeon Rock as the most likely spot to look. Marble spent 12 years digging, blasting and digging some more, searching for the pirate's gold he believed to be hidden in the cave. He dug until his death in 1868, and after he died his son Edwin dug for a few more years. Although the 7-foot-wide tunnel eventually reached a length of 150 feet, their efforts were fruitless and no treasure was ever found. The tunnel is still there, and if you walk into the crevice of Dungeon Rock you can see the metal door that marks its entrance.

After viewing Dungeon Rock, continue STRAIGHT on the dirt road.

1.2   Turn RIGHT onto a dirt road (Burrill Hill Road).

1.7   At the top of a hill, you pass a stone tower on the right.
This octagonal edifice, looking like the misplaced turret of a medieval castle, marks the top of Burrill Hill. At 283 feet, Burrill Hill is the highest point in Lynn Woods and was crowned with this 55-foot

tower in 1936. Disappointingly, the stairs inside the tower are unsafe, so you have to settle for imagining how nice the view must be from its top.

1.9 At the bottom of a hill, bear RIGHT as you join in with another dirt road. Part of the next section of the ride is on narrow, rocky trail. If you prefer a shorter ride that stays on the easier dirt roads, turn left here and skip to the directions at mile 5.5. You will be at the fork those directions refer to.

2.1 As you approach the end of a pond on the left (Walden Pond), turn LEFT onto a dirt path that runs between the pond and a small brick building on the right. After 70 yards, turn LEFT at the end of the path onto a dirt road. Continue on this dirt road as it runs along the right side of the pond. (Ox Pasture Road).

Walden Pond was built in 1889 as a water supply for Lynn. Unlike the more famous pond that shares its name, this Walden Pond was not named by a philosopher such as Thoreau, but by a chairman of the Water Board—Edwin Walden.

2.7 At a clearing on the left by the edge of the lake, bear LEFT onto a path marked by white blazes (Overlook Trail). Continue on this trail, following the white blazes.

The white-blazed Overlook Trail is narrow, rocky and steep in parts. There are a number of other trails that run parallel to the Overlook Trail and provide better riding, but none of them are clearly marked. If you are willing to explore, however, you can find alternate routes that avoid some of the difficult or unrideable sections of the Overlook Trail.

3.5 As you reach the top of a bare rock-outcrop, the white-blazed trail forks. An arrow painted on the rock marks the left fork B and the right fork P. Bear LEFT and continue following the white blazes.

Along this part of the ride are some of the rock formations for which Lynn Woods is famous. The hills in Lynn Woods are part of a chain of granite knobs that run just inland of the Massachusetts coast from Rockport to Quincy. As the glaciers of the last ice age retreated, they dropped huge boulders, known as glacial erratics, all over the countryside. When these boulders were left in rocky terrain like that of Lynn Woods, they often ended up perched precariously on one another in strange formations. Among them are Balanced Boulder, a huge erratic sitting on a rock ledge; Great Frog Boulder, which resembles a frog with its mouth open ready to snap a fly; and Cannon Rock, a large boulder balanced on three small stones.

3.9 As the white-blazed trail reaches a T intersection with a dirt road (Ox Pasture Road), turn RIGHT onto this road, continuing to follow the white blazes.

4.0   As the white-blazed trail turns left onto a dirt path, continue STRAIGHT on the dirt road. You will no longer be following the white blazes.

At this intersection there is a grassy path that leads back sharply to the left. Ten yards up this path on the right are the wolf pits — two long, narrow pits lined with stones. These were dug in the early 1600's and used to trap the wolves that once roamed the forests of New England and which were a scourge to the early settlers, killing their valuable livestock. A pit was covered with brush and then sprinkled with bait to attract a wolf. Once trapped, the animal could not escape and was thus easily killed. Used often in colonial times, wolf pits such as these two must have been effective, since wolves are now extinct in New England.

5.3   As you reach the end of the pond, turn RIGHT onto a path that runs between the pond and a small brick building on the left. After 70 yards, turn RIGHT at the end of this path onto a dirt road (Great Woods Road).

5.5   At a fork, bear RIGHT.

6.1   Just after passing the remnants of a stone wall on the right, two dirt roads lead up to the left. Turn LEFT on the first of these roads.

6.4   You reach the top of Mount Gilead, marked by a rusted steel tower. Here you have a good view of the Boston skyline and the coast. Continue STRAIGHT on the road past the tower and down the hill.

6.6   At a T intersection, turn RIGHT and continue down the hill.

6.8   At a T intersection at the bottom of the hill, turn LEFT. Continue on this road (Great Woods Road to Pennybrook Road) as it runs along the shore of a pond on the right (Walden Pond) and then across the park.

8.0   Bear LEFT as you join in with another road coming in from the right.

9.0   You are back at the western gate, where the tour began.

Additional Information
Lynn Parks Department, Lynn City Hall, Lynn, MA (617-598-4000).
The Friends of Lynn Woods, P.O. Box 8216, Lynn, MA 01904.

Bicycle Service
Lynn Shore Cycle, 251 Western Avenue, Lynn (617-581-2700). Sales, service.
Northeast Bicycles and Skis, 102 Broadway, Saugus (617-233-2664). Sales, service.

Middlesex Fells

Distance: 8.0 miles
Terrain: Bridle path, rolling, with a few larger hills
Difficulty: Easy to moderate
Map: Middlesex Fells (available at the Middlesex Fells Reservation Office); USGS 7.5′ × 15′ Boston North

> Hardly a fifteen minute ride, as the automobile flies, from the very gates of the State House lies today a domain of another century. In the heart of the most thickly settled part of Massachusetts is set apart forever for its people the charming reservation known as the Middlesex Fells. Primitive it cannot be. . . . It lies too close to us to be fully appreciated, but if one knows the art of horsemanship or the rarer art of walking, the Middlesex Fells is still a land of romance.

These words, from a 1935 article in the Medford Historical Register, ring as true today as when they were written. The Fells is still a land of romance, a wild tract of craggy rock-strewn forest, hills and ponds sprawling over 2,100 acres only five miles from downtown Boston. The land is wild, but hardly a wilderness; its forests have been cut down and replanted, its rivers and streams buried and dammed and its trails bisected by an interstate highway. Despite these setbacks, the Fells has retained much of its character. In fact, exploring it for the first time can be a revelation, making one wonder how so much land has been spared the fate of the suburban development that has befallen the area around it. For many Greater Boston residents, the Fells provides a much-needed escape from the urban rat race after a long day of work, a small piece of nature to enjoy when there's no time to travel farther.

The Fells has always been a locale valued for its natural resources. Made up of land taken from Medford, Stoneham, Malden, Melrose and Winchester, the Fells was created as a park in 1894, when it was given its name from a Saxon word meaning "a tract of wild stone hills." But even before it was a park, the unique geography of the Fells set it apart from the land around it. Its first use came with early settlers, who divided it into woodlots and harvested its trees for firewood. As these settlers became established, they developed industries, and the Fells provided the raw materials to support them. In the 1700's, Medford became famous

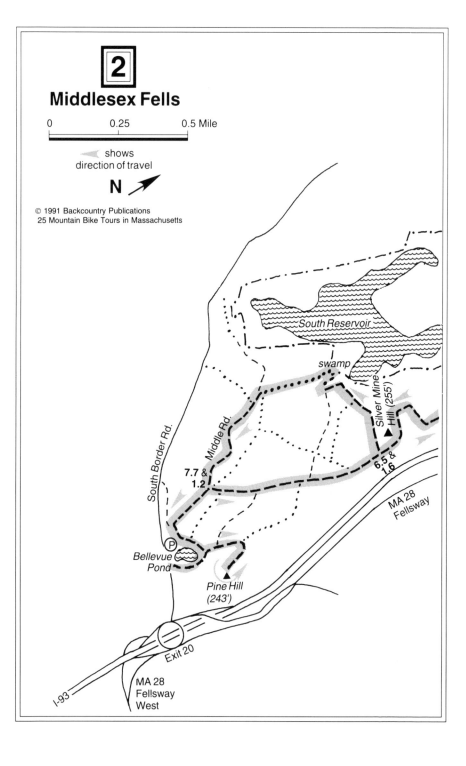

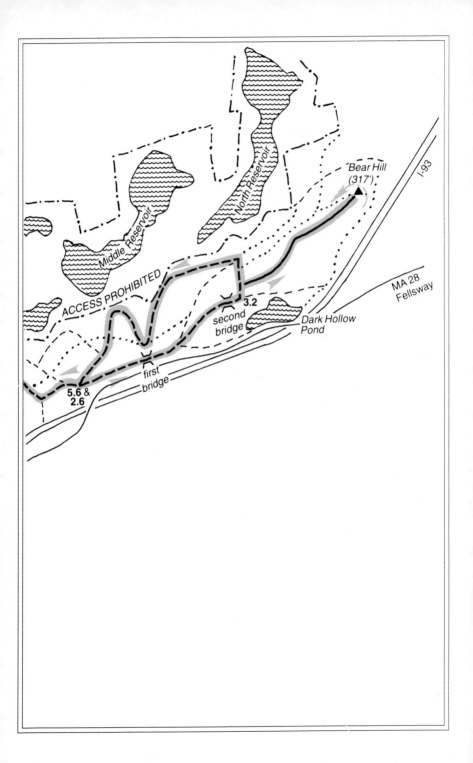

around the world for its rum production, with trees from the Fells firing the stills. In the 1800's, oak and pine taken from the Fells helped to establish Medford as a major shipbuilding center. Mills for the production of snuff, chocolate and spices were built to take advantage of the water power in the streams of the Fells, ice was harvested from its ponds, and granite cut from its quarries. There was even a village, Haywardville, that grew up around a rubber mill built by Elisha Converse and taken over by Nathaniel Hayward, a pioneer in the production of vulcanized rubber. The village as well as evidence of other industries have since disappeared. Through extensive reforestation in the early twentieth century the Fells has been restored to its natural state, or at least to a modern facsimile thereof.

Today the Fells is a popular recreation area frequented by hikers, equestrians, picnickers, cross country skiers and mountain bikers. Crossed by bridle paths, fire roads, and hiking trails, it is heavily used by mountain bikers. Because of erosion caused by overuse, mountain bikes are not allowed on the hiking trails. There is still plenty of good riding on the bridle paths and fire roads. Even in these areas, extra care must be taken to prevent trail damage, and riding in the Fells should be avoided during the spring mud season. If you encounter mud while riding, resist the temptation to ride through it, or even worse, around it, as doing so widens mudholes and trail blow-outs. Take the extra care to stop and walk your bike around the mud; it's a small price to pay for continued access to this area. You should also avoid riding near the Winchester reservoirs in the center of the Fells, as they are town water supplies. Their boundaries are clearly marked with No Trespassing signs, and are often patrolled: if you are caught riding near them you may be fined. Since the Fells trail policy may change, please check with the MDC office (address below) before riding to inquire about current trail restrictions.

To Get There: From I-93, take exit 20 for MA 28, Fellsway West, Stoneham. The exit ramp leads into a traffic circle. Continue around the circle, then turn right onto South Border Road. Continue on South Border Road for 0.2 mile, then turn right into a parking area by a pond.

The Ride

Except for the section of road that leads up to and back from Bear Hill, the entire route of this ride is marked by diamond-shaped, blue plastic blazes that make it easy to follow. At a few points, the trail doubles back on itself at forks with blue blazes leading off in both directions. Consult the written directions at these points. Also, be sure not to confuse the blue plastic blazes that mark this ride with the blue paint blazes you might also see.

0.0   The ride begins at the parking area on South Border Road. Start down

Middlesex Fells

the dirt path that runs along the right side of Bellevue Pond, marked by diamond-shaped blue plastic blazes.

0.1   At the end of the pond, the blue plastic blazes lead in two directions, one branch turning left and the other continuing straight. Continue STRAIGHT, following the blue plastic blazes and the sign for Pine Hill Overlook as the path turns to the right and climbs to the top of Pine Hill.

At the top of Pine Hill is Wright Tower, built in honor of Elizur Wright, the founder of Middlesex Fells. Wright, a man of diverse talents, was a conservationist, a vocal anti-slavery activist and the founder of the life insurance business. In 1869, he began lobbying for the creation of a private park in the area of the Fells, known at that time as Five-Mile Wood. He continued his efforts for 16 years, raising money to buy property and getting legislation passed to preserve forest lands. After his death in 1885, his work was continued by others until 1894, when his vision became reality with the creation of the Middlesex Fells Reservation. The land around Pine Hill, which had been the site of Wright's estate, was donated to the reservation by Wright's children in memory of their father.

Climb to the top of the tower for a view of the events of the distant and not so distant past that have shaped the Fells. As you look down, notice the contour of Pine Hill, smooth on one side and rough on the other. During the last ice age, glaciers moving across New England toward the south smoothed down the north side of the hill. But when the ice moved over the hill, it froze to the rock and pulled it away, leaving jagged cliffs on its southern side and dropping large boulders at random over the landscape. Since being formed by the last ice age, the hill has endured the ravages of man's movement across the landscape. In 1775, all the timber on Pine Hill was cleared to supply Washington's army with lumber. The forest regrew, but was stripped again for lumber in 1855. Since then, the new growth has been left uncut; however, it has suffered periodic attacks from gypsy moth caterpillars and been subjected to air pollution from nearby I-93, built through the middle of the Fells in the 1960's.

0.5 From the top of Pine Hill, return the way you came, following the blue plastic blazes back to Bellevue Pond.

0.8 Just before you reach a stone wall by Bellevue Pond, turn RIGHT, following the blue plastic blazes on a path around the pond. Continue following the blue plastic blazes as the trail winds through the woods and turns right onto a wider path.

1.2 At a fork with a sign marked Middle Road, the blue plastic blazes lead both left and right. Bear RIGHT and continue following the blue plastic blazes.

1.6 At a fork, the blue plastic blazes again lead both left and right. Bear RIGHT, following the signs marked Silver Mine Connector and Silver Mine Path, and continue following the blue plastic blazes.

"Thar's gold in them thar Fells!" In 1881, on a nearby hill, excitement came to the Fells when a prospector dug a 30-foot mine shaft and found 18 dollars worth of silver, 4 dollars of gold and large amounts of copper. For the next two years this silver mine was worked, the shaft being sunk to 85 feet with dirt and debris hauled up from the bottom by windlass and bucket. These efforts ended up being fruitless, and the mine was abandoned after a great deal of money had been sunk into it.

2.6   At a fork with a sign marked Silver Mine Connector, Bellevue Pond Loop, the blue plastic blazes again lead both left and right. Bear RIGHT. In 0.1 mile, as you come close to a road on the right, follow the blue plastic blaze marked with an arrow onto a parallel path which crosses over a bridge. Continue following the blue plastic blazes.

3.2   Just after crossing a second bridge, turn LEFT following a blue plastic blaze with an arrow on it. Turn immediately RIGHT onto a crumbling paved road, which is a spur trail to Bear Hill. This part of the trail is not marked with blue plastic blazes. Follow this road to the top of Bear Hill, where there is a water tower and an observation tower.

Bear Hill, at 317 feet, is the highest point in the Fells. Climb the spiral staircase to the top of the hexagonal observatory for a comprehensive view of the Fells, the Greater Boston area, and on a clear day, a good part of southern New England. From the tower, you get a clear view of the ring of hills that surround the flat plain of Greater Boston, an area known as the Boston Basin. The floor of the basin is composed of slate, a soft rock formed long ago when eastern Massachusetts was under the Atlantic Ocean. During millions of years of erosion the slate was worn down more quickly than the hard granite hills surrounding it, forming the basin you see before you. This action was aided by earthquakes that periodically dropped the level of the basin, and are still occasionally felt. The Fells sits just on the northern edge of the basin, and a major fault line runs along the south edge of the reservation. The southern rim of the Boston Basin is marked by the Blue Hills, which you can see due south 17 miles away. Other landmarks visible from the tower are Mount Wachusett, 40 miles to the west, and north of that Mount Monadnock in southern New Hampshire. To the east, along the ocean, Revere Beach and the Nahant peninsula are visible, and farther out you may just be able to espy the outer reaches of Cape Cod.

3.8   Return back the way you came down Bear Hill.

4.5   At the intersection with the blue-blazed path, turn RIGHT, then bear LEFT at the next fork, once again following the blue plastic blazes.

5.6   At the sign marked Silver Mine Connector, Bellevue Pond Loop, you rejoin the path you started out on. Continue following the blue plastic blazes.

6.5   At a fork with a sign marked Bellevue Pond Loop 2.7 mi., the blue plastic blazes lead both left and right. Bear RIGHT, following the sign marked East Dam Road. Continue following the blue plastic blazes.

6.8   After a sharp left turn marked by a blue plastic blaze with an arrow, the path narrows to a trail that winds steeply down a hill to a swampy area. At the bottom of the hill, cross the swampy area on the logs laid across the mud and continue following the blue plastic blazes on the other side of the swamp as the trail climbs through the woods and then turns left onto a wider path. In order to avoid trail damage, walk your bike along this narrow section of trail until you have rejoined the wider path.

7.7   The path rejoins the path you started out on. Bear RIGHT and continue following the blue plastic blazes back the way you came.

8.0   You are back at the parking lot at Bellevue Pond, where the ride began.

Additional Information

Middlesex Fells Reservation Office, 1 Woodland Road, Stoneham, MA 02180 (617-662-5214). Monday to Friday, 8:00 a.m.–4:00 p.m. Trail maps may be purchased at the office for $2.00 or by mail for $2.50.

Bicycle Service

City Cycle, 286 Main Street, Stoneham (617-438-0358). Sales, service.

Malden Cycle Center, 77 Commercial Street, Malden (617-322-1880). Sales, service.

Pro Cycles, 515 Main Street, Melrose (617-662-2813). Sales, service.

More Rides Near Boston

This chapter gives a brief description of four additional places to ride around Greater Boston, areas that were either too small for a full chapter, or were in the process of defining their mountain biking trail-use policies at the time this book was written. Although small, all offer interesting trails and are conveniently located within or just outside the MA 128 loop.

Blue Hills Reservation

Blue Hills Reservation, 6,500 acres of woodlands stretching across Dedham, Quincy, Milton and Randolph, is one of the most popular places to mountain bike in Greater Boston. The largest park operated by the Metropolitan District Commission (MDC) and the largest open space within 35 miles of Boston, the reservation is traversed by a seemingly endless network of trails and bridle paths. These vary from flat, wide and smooth to narrow, rocky and steep, and riders of all abilities should be able to find something to suit them. Given its size, with some planning it's possible to put together long, interesting rides that run from one end of the reservation to the other.

Blue Hills has long been a favorite spot for hikers and horseback riders, and in recent years its use by mountain bikers has increased steadily. Because of this, the MDC has been studying the impact of mountain bikes on the trail system. At the time this book was being written, mountain biking in the Blue Hills Reservation was restricted to fire roads only. Riding at Blue Hills should also be avoided during the spring mud season. Since this policy may change, please check with the MDC office at the Blue Hills Reservation headquarters before riding to inquire about their current trail policy.

If you do ride at Blue Hills, remember that your actions as a rider have a great deal to do with shaping future trail policy. If mountain bikers prove to be responsible trail users, restrictions will be minimized; otherwise, mountain bikes may be prohibited from the reservation. Be sure to ride in control at all times, and yield the trail to other users. Slow down to pass hikers, and remember that when approaching a horse from the front, a mountain biker should stop and move off the trail until the horse passes. When approaching a horse from behind, call ahead to the rider from a safe distance to make sure it's okay to pass.

The size of Blue Hills Reservation and the number of trails that

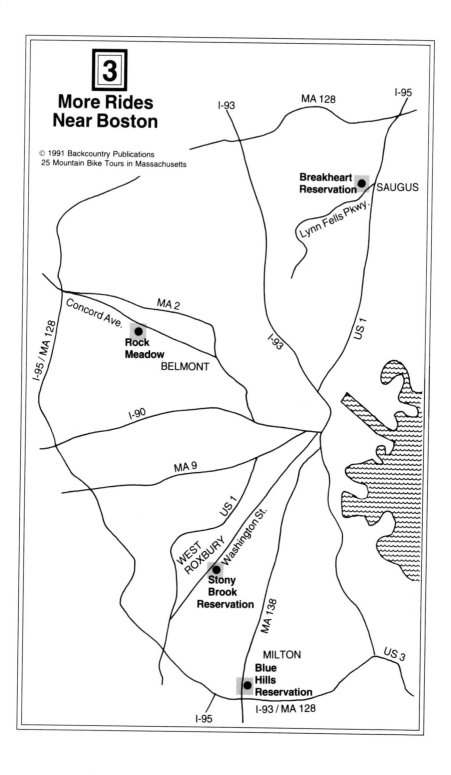

3
More Rides
Near Boston

© 1991 Backcountry Publications
25 Mountain Bike Tours in Massachusetts

MA 128   I-95

I-93

Breakheart
Reservation   SAUGUS

Lynn Fells Pkwy.

Concord Ave.   MA 2

I-95 / MA 128

US 1

Rock
Meadow

BELMONT

I-93

I-90

MA 9

US 1

Washington St.

WEST
ROXBURY

Stony
Brook
Reservation

MA 138

MILTON

US 3

Blue
Hills
Reservation

I-95   I-93 / MA 128

crisscross it make it an easy place in which to get lost. If you plan to venture out for any significant distance, it is a good idea to get both maps listed below, as each shows a slightly different view of the trails in the reservation. Together, both maps will give you a more complete picture of the trail system.

Map: Blue Hills Reservation Trail Map and Guide (available at reservation office); Neponset River and the Blue Hills Reservation (available at Trailside Museum)

To Get There: From MA 128 take exit 2B, MA 138 North, Milton. Follow MA 138 North for 0.4 mile to the first traffic light. At this point you may either turn right at the traffic light onto Hillside Street and park in one of the lots which you will pass in the next mile, or continue straight on MA 138 for 0.8 mile and park in the lot at the Trailside Museum, which is just past the ski area. It is best to avoid the parking lot at the Trailside Museum on weekends as it tends to be crowded. The parking lots along Hillside Street will put you closer to some of the more remote and less frequently visited parts of the reservation.

Additional Information
Blue Hills Reservation Headquarters (MDC office), 695 Hillside Street, Milton, MA (617-698-1802).
Blue Hills Trailside Museum, MA 138, Milton, MA (617-333-0690). Open Sunday–Tuesday, 10:00 a.m. to 5:00 p.m. Admission $3.00 adults, $1.50 children.
Blue Hills Mountain Bike Committee, c/o Joe Sloane, 6 Francis Street, Milton, MA 02186 (617-696-2046).

Bicycle Service
Steve's Bike Barn, 1030 Pleasant Street, Canton (617-828-8146). Sales, service.
Dedham Bike and Leather, 403 Washington Street, Dedham (617-326-1531). Sales, service, rentals.

Stony Brook Reservation

Stony Brook Reservation, the only place to ride off-road within the city of Boston, is an oasis of woodlands in a desert of urban sprawl. The reservation is not well known, and many people who come across it by chance are surprised to find so many trees surviving in such inhospitable surroundings. The reservation's 450 acres, located in the southwest corner of the city near West Roxbury, Roslindale and Hyde Park, are managed by the MDC as part of the Metropolitan Parks System, a chain of parks running throughout the Greater Boston area.

Stony Brook Reservation is packed with bridle paths, forest trails and a paved bike path, and is bisected by the Turtle Pond Parkway, which must be crossed (carefully) to reach all the trails. The terrain is rolling, with the trails generally running downhill north to south. Its nu-

merous hills give the reservation a roughhewn texture that, despite its compactness, nevertheless offers some interesting and challenging riding.

Map: USGS 7.5′ × 15′ Newton

To Get There: From MA 128 (I-95), take exit 15A for US 1 North, Dedham. Follow US 1 North for 1.6 miles, then bear right onto Washington Street. Follow Washington Street for 2.2 miles, then turn right onto LaGrange. Park in the lot at the corner of Washington and LaGrange, or continue on LaGrange to the Turtle Pond Parkway and park in one of the lots alongside it. To reach the trails from the corner of Washington and

LaGrange, continue on LaGrange toward the woods. After 70 yards, turn left on the Turtle Pond Parkway (crossing with caution), and in 75 yards turn right onto a dirt path marked Bearberry Hill Road.

Additional Information
Metropolitan District Commission, 20 Somerset Street, Boston, MA (617-727-5215).

Bicycle Service
Ferris Wheels Bicycle Shop, 64 South Street, Jamaica Plain (617-522-7082). Sales, service.

Weston Conservation Land

Located just west of MA 128 and north of I-90, the town of Weston is known as one of the more affluent and conveniently located bedroom communities in Greater Boston. What few people may know, however, is that this suburban town has done a superb job of preserving open space within its borders. There are over 2200 acres of public open land in Weston, crossed by 65 miles of trails. These trails are maintained by the Weston Forest and Trail Association. Formed in 1955, the Association was one of the first groups in Massachusetts dedicated to protecting open land for public use. Along with maintaining trails, the Association runs trail walks and sponsors lectures with the goal of educating the public on the value of preserving and maintaining conservation land.

Like many trails in densely populated areas, the trails in Weston see heavy use by a range of user groups. Because of this, mountain bikers should be especially careful to obey the rules of the trail: limit riding to fire roads, ride slowly, yield to hikers and equestrians, respect private property, and stay off the trails when they are wet.

The trails in Weston are located on numerous small parcels of land. Many of these parcels are connected by trails and roads, so that shorter rides can easily be connected into a longer loop. With the variety of trails in town, the best place to start a ride in Weston is at the Weston Town Hall, where maps of the trail network are sold.

Map: Town of Weston Massachusetts, 1993. Available at Weston Town Hall for $10.

To Get There: To get to the Weston Town Hall: From MA 128 (I-95), take exit 26 for MA 20 West. Follow MA 20 West for 1.4 miles, then turn right at a traffic light onto School Street. In 0.1 mile, continue straight across an intersection, then immediately bear right. In 0.1 mile, turn left onto Town House Road. The Weston Town Hall is a brick building with white pillars on the right. Maps are sold in an office in the town hall basement.

Bicycle Service

Belmont Wheel Works, 480 Trapelo Road, Belmont (617-489-3577). Sales, service.

Breakheart Reservation

Breakheart Reservation is a 600-acre preserve in Saugus and Wakefield managed by the MDC. The terrain is studded with steep, craggy hills, none of which is more than a few hundred feet high, but since many have treeless crests they provide surprisingly good views of the surrounding landscape.

The trails at Breakheart are best for experienced riders, those who enjoy the challenge of slowly maneuvering up, down and around rocks, roots and fallen trees. Although there was once a network of fire roads through the reservation, most of these have been paved over; the dirt trails that remain tend to be narrow, rocky and difficult. The trails that circle the two lakes are relatively flat, but covered with slippery roots and closely spaced rocks that demand precise bike handling. Those that run along the outer edges of the reservation are hillier, with frequent short, steep climbs and corresponding drops. Often, these trails climb up and down rock faces that are impossible to ride and sometimes even difficult to carry a bike over.

At the time this book was being written, the MDC had not yet defined a policy for the use of mountain bikes in Breakheart Reservation. It is possible that they will create such a policy in the future, so you should call the reservation headquarters to inquire about their current trail policy. Also note that in order to prevent erosion damage, you should avoid riding at Breakheart during spring mud season and during or after a heavy rain.

Map: Breakheart Reservation (available at reservation office)

To Get There: From MA 128 (I-95) take exit 44A, US 1 South, Everett, Boston. Follow US 1 South for 2.6 miles, then take the exit for Lynn Fells Parkway, Melrose, Stoneham. Follow the Parkway for 0.3 mile, then turn left onto Forest Street at the sign for Breakheart Reservation. Follow Forest Street for 0.3 mile, then turn left into the parking lot at the reservation headquarters.

Additional Information
Breakheart Reservation, 177 Forest Street, Saugus, MA (617-233-0834).

Bicycle Service
Northeast Bicycles and Skis, 102 Broadway, Saugus (617-233-2664). Sales, service.
Wakefield Schwinn Cyclery, 16 Albion Street, Wakefield (617-245-2342). Sales, service.
Winters Bike Shop, 1116 Main Street, Wakefield (617-245-3515). Sales, service.

Bradley Palmer State Park and Willowdale State Forest

Distance: 17.2 miles
Terrain: Flat to rolling dirt path, with some connecting pavement
Difficulty: Moderate
Map: Bradley Palmer State Park, Willowdale State Forest (available at Bradley Palmer headquarters); USGS 7.5′ × 15′ Ipswich

What do you have to do to have a state park named after you? The answer is easy. Simply be wealthy enough to buy up vast tracts of land during your lifetime and be philanthropic enough to donate the land to the state when you die. Bradley Palmer had the formula down. With money earned during a successful career as a lawyer, he purchased over 3,000 acres of land in Topsfield and Ipswich and built his estate there. After his death, Palmer willed the property to the state of Massachusetts, which subsequently turned it into the Bradley Palmer State Park and Willowdale State Forest. Today, these two reservations, which preserve precious open space in the otherwise fenced-off hills of Essex County, stand as a testament both to Palmer's prosperity and to his generosity.

Bradley Palmer, originally from Wilkes Barre, Pennsylvania, settled in Boston after graduating from Harvard University around 1887 and Harvard Law School a few years later. He joined a law firm and built a successful practice, eventually becoming a partner and achieving considerable wealth. Palmer enjoyed the country life, and in the early 1900's he purchased the Lamson Farm in Topsfield from Mr. and Mrs. Lamson, whose family had owned the land since the seventeenth century. They were no longer able to work the farm, but when Palmer purchased it from them, he guaranteed them the right to stay in their house for the rest of their lives.

Palmer immediately set about improving the property. He built a stone house and stables, garages, farm buildings, a cottage for his superintendent, and a boat house and bridge by the river. To beautify the grounds, he had a freight car-load of rhododendron and laurel shipped from Pennsylvania. He also purchased a large stretch of land across the Ipswich River that had been cut for lumber in the late 1800's and then abandoned. He opened up old roads through this property and cut new ones for bridle paths. Palmer, who never married, was an enthusiastic equestrian and spent summers on his estate riding and hunting. He kept a stable of hunters and often rode with the Myopia Hunt Club in Hamilton, which he founded with a few other friends. He also laid out a steeplechase course on his estate, and the annual Myopia Steeplechase was held there.

Several years before his death in 1946, Palmer gave all his land north of the Ipswich River to the state, which turned it into the Willowdale State Forest. He offered the land south of the river to his sisters, who did not want it, and to the Audubon Society, which also declined, so he gave that to the state also. This land became the Bradley Palmer State Park. The buildings of Palmer's estate, as well as the old Lamson farmhouse, still stand and can be seen at the park.

This ride traverses the length of both Bradley Palmer State Park and Willowdale State Forest. It starts on a loop through Bradley Palmer, then crosses the Ipswich River over a wooden footbridge into Willowdale. It goes through Willowdale's three separate tracts, each connected to the next by a short distance of pavement. After reaching the far end of Willowdale State Forest, the tour returns to the start along paved roads.

In addition to the route covered on this ride there are many other trails to explore in both Bradley Palmer and Willowdale. There are also some interesting possibilities for long-distance touring. Within riding distance to the west of Willowdale are the Georgetown–Rowley State Forest, Boxford State Forest and Harold Parker State Forest. By connecting the trails in each of these woodlands with short stretches of pavement, it is possible to ride almost entirely off-road from Ipswich to Andover.

To Get There: From MA 1 in Topsfield, turn onto Ipswich Road at the sign for Bradley Palmer State Park. Follow Ipswich Road for 1.3 miles, then turn right onto Asbury Road at the sign for Bradley Palmer State Park. In 0.2 mile, turn left into the state park. Continue straight on the road which runs into the park following signs to the headquarters. Park in any one of the lots near the headquarters.

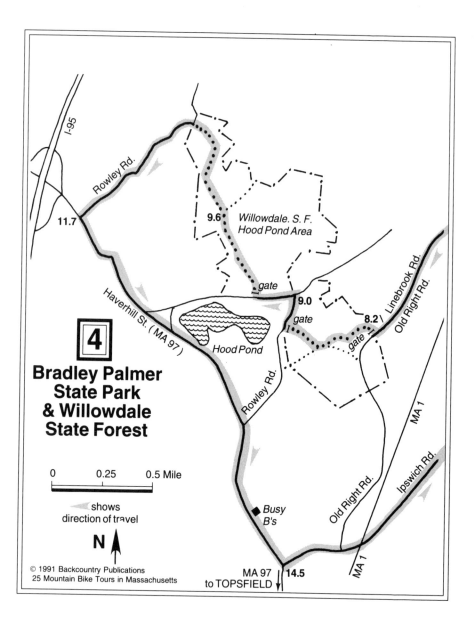

(In the image:)

I-95

Rowley Rd.

11.7

9.6 *Willowdale. S. F. Hood Pond Area*

Haverhill St. (MA 97)

gate

9.0

gate

8.2

gate

Linebrook Rd.

Old Right Rd.

4

Bradley Palmer State Park & Willowdale State Forest

Hood Pond

Rowley Rd.

MA 1

Old Right Rd.

Ipswich Rd.

0   0.25   0.5 Mile

shows direction of travel

N

© 1991 Backcountry Publications
25 Mountain Bike Tours in Massachusetts

◆ *Busy B's*

MA 97
to TOPSFIELD

14.5

MA 1

The Ride

0.0 The ride begins directly in front of the state park headquarters. Start down the paved road which runs from the front of the headquarters toward the horse van area.

0.1 At a signboard on the left showing a map of Massachusetts State Forests

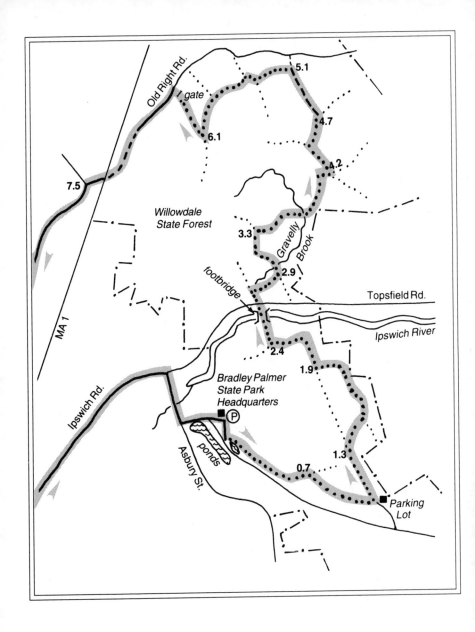

and Parks, turn LEFT onto a dirt path which runs alongside a pond on the right. Continue on this path past trails intersecting left and right.

As you ride along this section of trail, look for the mountain laurel and rhododendron that Bradley Palmer imported and planted around his estate. The mountain laurel has a broad, flat leaf with a waxy covering that helps it retain water. This coating enables the laurel to live in dry, rocky conditions and to stay green all winter. The rhododendron's leaves are of similar shape to the mountain laurel's, and it is also an evergreen. When blooming, rhododendron flowers are recognizable by the cluster of dark spots in their center. These spots serve as a target to guide insects to the plant's sweet nectar.

0.7   As the dirt path forks, bear RIGHT.

1.0   As the dirt path turns to pavement and runs into a parking lot, continue STRAIGHT across the parking lot. At the end of the parking lot, turn LEFT onto a dirt path which passes through a wooden fence and runs across an open field.

1.3   As you come to another wooden fence in the center of the field, bear RIGHT at a fork. Continue on this trail as it runs uphill into the woods.

1.5   As a trail joins in from the right, bear LEFT and continue uphill.

1.9   As you come down a small hill to an open field marked by an L-shaped wooden fence, turn RIGHT at a T intersection.

2.4   As the trail completes a wide U turn to the left, watch for three large logs lying perpendicular to the trail on the right. At these logs, turn RIGHT onto a path marked by a red paint blaze as it enters the woods.

2.5   Continue STRAIGHT across a wooden footbridge over the Ipswich River. After 50 yards, cross a paved road (Ipswich Road) and continue STRAIGHT on a dirt path into the Willowdale State Forest.

The Ipswich River was called Agawam, "resort for fish of passage," by the Indians. Its source is in the hills of Burlington and it meanders for 25 miles until it reaches the Atlantic at its namesake town. The earliest recorded description of the river was given in 1646 by Captain Edward Johnson, the town clerk of Woburn, who described it as,

> A faire and delightful river, whose first rise or spring begins about twenty-five miles farther up the country, issuing forth a very pleasant pond. But soon after it betakes its course through a most hideous swamp of large extent, even for many miles, being a great harbour for bears. After its coming forth this place, it groweth larger by the income of many small rivers, and issues forth in the sea, due east against the Island of Sholes, a great place for fishing for our English nation.

The swamp that Johnson mentions is just upstream from the point at which you stand; the river "issues forth into the sea" six or so miles downstream from this spot.

The abundance of fish in the river and the fertile soil surround-

ing it made the land around the Ipswich an attractive place for the early colonists. The Pilgrims considered it a likely spot to settle, as indicated by the words of some of the *Mayflower's* crew who "urged greatly the going to Agawam, or Angawam, a place twenty leagues off to the Northward, which they heard to be an excellent harbour for ships, better ground and better fishing." Had this suggestion been heeded, the river you are crossing now would just as likely be called the Plymouth instead of the Ipswich.

2.6   Just after entering Willowdale, at the bottom of a small hill bear RIGHT at a fork.

2.9 At a T intersection, turn LEFT. Continue STRAIGHT as the trail crosses a brook (Gravelly Brook) and continues through the woods.

3.3 At a fork, bear RIGHT.

4.2 At an intersection where two trails lead off to the right, bear LEFT to stay on the trail as it curves sharply to the left.

4.5 At a fork where a grassy path leads off to the left, bear RIGHT to stay on the dirt path.

4.7 At a T intersection marked by a red blaze with a white maple leaf, turn LEFT onto a wide dirt road.

5.1 At a fork where the main dirt path continues straight, bear LEFT on a narrow dirt path marked by a large orange circle on a tree 30 yards down the trail.

5.5 At a fork, bear RIGHT, and after 150 yards, at a fork, bear LEFT.

5.9 At a fork, bear LEFT.

6.1 At a fork, bear RIGHT.

6.5 Pass though a gate and turn LEFT onto a paved road (Old Right Road).

6.7 Continue STRAIGHT as the paved road turns to dirt.

7.3 At a four-way intersection, cross a paved road (MA 1) and continue STRAIGHT on Old Right Road, which is now paved.

7.5 At a fork, bear LEFT.

8.2 At a yellow wire gate on the right, turn RIGHT onto a dirt path.

8.4 At a fork, bear RIGHT.

8.8 At the end of the dirt path, go through a yellow wire gate and turn RIGHT onto a paved road (Rowley Road).

9.0 At a T intersection, turn LEFT (Linebrook Road).

9.2 At a yellow wire gate on the right, turn RIGHT onto a dirt path.

9.6 At a fork, bear LEFT.

10.8 As the dirt path ends, turn LEFT on a paved road (Rowley Road).

11.7 At a T intersection, turn LEFT (MA 97).
    If you wish, you may ride on the paved bike paths that run parallel to the road for much of the way back to Bradley Palmer.

14.2 You pass the Busy B's takeout stand on the left. If you're hungry, stop here and knock back a tall, cool glass of lemonade and some of their world-famous french fries and coleslaw.

14.5 At an intersection, turn back sharply to the LEFT onto Ipswich Road. Continuing straight at this intersection will bring you into Topsfield Center. This well-preserved New England town is well worth visiting if you have time.

15.4 At a traffic signal, cross MA 1 and continue STRAIGHT.

16.7 At the sign for Bradley Palmer State Park, turn RIGHT (Asbury Street).

17.0 Turn LEFT into Bradley Palmer State Park and follow the access road back to park headquarters.

17.2 You are back at the state park headquarters, where the tour began.

Additional Information
Bradley Palmer State Park, Asbury Street, Topsfield, MA (508-887-5931).

Bicycle Service
Skol Bicycle Shop, 26 Central Street, Ipswich (508-356-5872). Sales, service.
The Bicycle Shop, 17 Main Street, Topsfield (508-887-6511). Sales, service.

Dogtown

Distance: 10.8 miles
Terrain: Rolling dirt path and forest trail with occasional rocky sections and some connecting pavement
Difficulty: Moderate
Map: USGS 7.5′ × 15′ Rockport

Dogtown, the name given to the wooded interior of the Cape Ann peninsula north of Boston, is a strange name for a strange place. If you're a casual visitor to Dogtown, knowing nothing of its flea-bitten history, all you see at first is a hilly tract of boulder-strewn New England countryside. But when you're riding along, turn a corner and are confronted by a huge boulder carved with the cryptic message GET A JOB, you realize that there is more to Dogtown than at first appears. That's because Dogtown has a colorful history, with bits and pieces of that history still strewn about its fields and forests to be dug up like buried bones. Dogtown is a ghost town, the site of one of the first settlements on Cape Ann, abandoned over 200 years ago when its inhabitants moved closer to the coast. As you ride through Dogtown on a mountain bike, you combine a challenging ride over rocky forest trails with a chance to explore the remnants of a deserted New England village.

The story of Dogtown began in the early seventeenth century with the settlement of Cape Ann. Accustomed to a farm life in England, the first settlers of Gloucester established a village in the interior of the Cape where there was land to plant crops. The wooded areas near this settlement, called the Commons, were used as a grazing area and fuel supply. As the settlement grew and more space was needed for housing, the Commons were divided into house lots, and a village began to grow. In the early 1700's, up to 100 houses were built there and it became a desirable place to live, home to some of the best families in Gloucester.

Starting in the mid-eighteenth century, however, the fortunes of the Commons began to change when the residents of Gloucester realized that it was easier to make a living by fishing and trading than by farming the rocky New England soil. The wealthier families in town moved from the interior of Cape Ann to its coast in order to be closer to the source of this new commerce. The houses they moved out of on the Commons were rented out, often to poor people, widows and newcomers. The neglected houses gradually fell apart and the area became a shanty-town. Packs of dogs roamed the place, giving rise to the derogatory name, Dogtown.

For the next hundred years, the houses of Dogtown were occupied by the outcasts of Cape Ann society—characters of questionable pedigree, said to be witches, prostitutes, fortunetellers and eccentrics. It became a kind of red light district, with gossip and rumors giving rise to legends about the people who lived there. Eventually, all the houses in Dogtown fell apart or were knocked down, and its residents died or moved away; the last resident was carted off to the poorhouse in 1830.

Since then, Dogtown has remained uninhabited. Much of the land is now owned by the towns of Rockport and Gloucester and is preserved as conservation land. The area is crossed by a confusing maze of trails that vary from wide and smooth to narrow, rocky and unrideable. Some of the trails have been blazed, but there is no map available that shows all the trails. This ride follows the main trails which run from one end of Dogtown to the other, and then returns to the start on paved roads. There are many good trails to ride in Dogtown in addition to the ones covered here, but since there is no good map of the area it will take some exploring to find them.

To Get There: Follow MA 128 North to its second intersection with MA 127 in Gloucester. Turn left onto MA 127 North (Eastern Avenue) for 1.0 mile, then turn left onto Pond Street; marked by a sign for Morse Industrial Park. Limited parking is available on Pond Street. Be sure not to park in the private or business lots on Pond Street and obey any posted parking restrictions, as this area is heavily visited in summer and illegally parked cars may be towed.

The Ride

0.0   The ride begins at the corner of Pond Street and MA 127 (Eastern Avenue). From Pond Street, turn LEFT onto MA 127. Continue north on MA 127.

0.5   Watch for a metal gate on the left marked by orange and white stripes. Turn LEFT through this gate onto a dirt road (Old Rockport Road). Continue on this dirt road past paths intersecting from the left and right.

1.4   The dirt road widens, then ends at an embankment, continuing as a paved road on the other side. Bear RIGHT onto a dirt path that runs to the right of the embankment and then continues into the woods just to the right of a large metal tower.

1.5   Turn RIGHT on a path marked at its beginning by a pile of broken tiles. Continue on this path, bearing RIGHT at the next three forks. After a few hundred yards, you will see a boulder on your left inscribed with the words GET A JOB. Continue on this path as it narrows and winds down a steep hill to railroad tracks by a reservoir (Babson Reservoir). Watch for more carved boulders along the way.

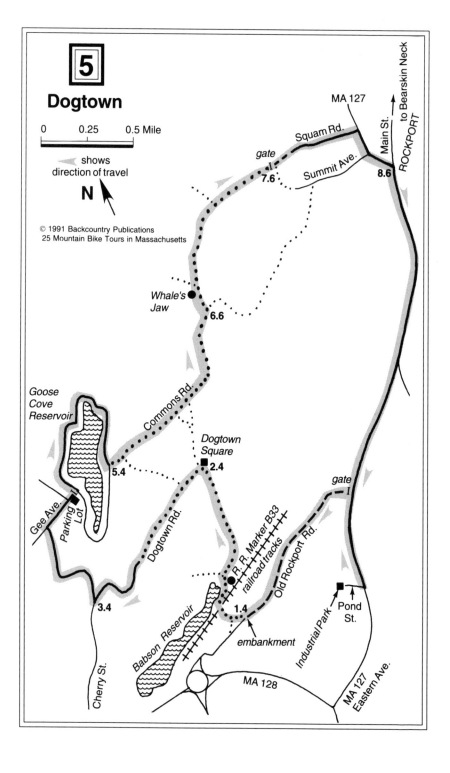

5

Dogtown

0   0.25   0.5 Mile

shows
direction of travel

N

© 1991 Backcountry Publications
25 Mountain Bike Tours in Massachusetts

to Bearskin Neck

ROCKPORT

MA 127

Main St.

Squam Rd.

gate

7.6

Summit Ave.

8.6

Whale's
Jaw

6.6

Goose
Cove
Reservoir

Commons Rd.

Dogtown
Square

2.4

5.4

Gee Ave.

Parking
Lot

Dogtown Rd.

gate

R. R. Marker B33

railroad tracks

Old Rockport Rd.

Industrial Park

Pond
St.

3.4

Babson Reservoir

1.4

embankment

Cherry St.

MA 128

MA 127
Eastern Ave.

The carved boulders you see throughout Dogtown are the work of Roger Babson. Born in 1875, Babson was a Gloucester native—founder of Babson College, financial wizard, unsuccessful presidential candidate and eccentric. He grew up in the area around Dogtown and came to love it, in later years donating 1,110 acres around Babson Reservoir to be preserved as conservation land and watershed. He also wrote extensively about the history of Dogtown and supervised the carving of the boulders. These boulders are of two types: 20 or so huge ones in the general vicinity of the reservoir with inspirational messages carved into them, and some 40 smaller rocks along Dogtown Road, Wharf Road and Commons Road, bearing numbers that mark former Dogtown house sites. In his book, *Cape Ann Tourist's Guide,* Babson matches the numbered house sites with the histories of their former inhabitants.

1.6   At the railroad tracks, turn RIGHT and follow the tracks. Be careful, as these are live tracks and trains may be passing.

1.7   Just before railroad marker B 33, turn LEFT on a trail that leads down to the reservoir. After 40 yards turn RIGHT onto a trail that leads away from the reservoir into the woods. After a short distance you will see a boulder carved with the message TRUTH; you will see more carved messages along the way. Continue on this narrow trail as it winds through the woods, up a hill and across an overgrown field. This section of the trail is very rocky and can be difficult to ride.

2.4   Ten yards after passing a boulder inscribed with the message BE ON TIME, turn LEFT at a T intersection onto a wide dirt path (Dogtown Road).

This intersection, know as Dogtown Square, was once the center of the village. As you ride down Dogtown Road, look for boulders along the side of the trail carved with numbers marking former house sites. Many of these boulders are overgrown and difficult to find, but some along the right side of the trail are still clearly visible. If you take some time to explore, it is possible to see the cellar holes that mark the remains of the deserted houses.

If you look carefully, along the left side of the road you will find boulder number 15, which marks the site of the Easter Carter house. The story of this house, typical of Dogtown, is recounted in *The Saga of Cape Ann* by Melvin Copeland:

On . . . Dogtown road, about a mile from Gravel Hill, stood the house where Easter (Esther) Carter lived in the decadent years of Dogtown. She is supposed to have come from England with her brother about 1741 and eventually arrived in Dogtown. She was a spinster who went out nursing. She was very poor, but she was kind and hospitable and widely known. . . . After she moved to the village at the harbor, her dwelling continued to be known as "the Easter Carter house." The next tenant was Becky Rich, who previously had lived at the foot of Gravel Hill. When her house there became so dilapidated as to be untenable, Becky was moved to Easter Carter's house. She also was known as Granny Rich and she had a daughter, Rachel Smith, who made a "dire drink" brewed from foxberry leaves, spruce tops, and other herbs, which she peddled in the village to make her customers feel "springish." "Aunt Rachel" often entertained parties of young people from Riverdale and Annisquam who visited her at the Easter Carter house on picnic excursions. She boiled cabbage and baked johnnycakes for them, told their fortunes from coffee grounds, and generally helped them to have a good time. . . . On the upper floor of Easter Carter's house "Old Ruth" lived for some years. She was a mulatto who presumably had been a slave. She also was known as "John Woodman." She usually was employed for building stone walls and other heavy outdoor work to which she had become accustomed when she was young. Since she did a man's work, she dressed accordingly. It was only when she went to the poorhouse to spend her last days that she began to wear a skirt, and that was by compulsion, not by her choice.

3.0   Continue STRAIGHT as the dirt road turns to pavement.

3.4   At the end of the road, turn RIGHT (Cherry Street).

4.0   At a T intersection, turn RIGHT (Gee Avenue).

4.1   As the road turns sharply left, bear RIGHT into a small parking lot, through a metal gate and onto a paved path. After 50 yards, turn LEFT at a T intersection by a reservoir (Goose Cove Reservoir). Continue on this paved path as it circles the reservoir.

5.4   Halfway around the reservoir, turn LEFT onto a wide dirt path heading away from the reservoir (Common Road). After 150 yards, bear LEFT at a fork.

Look for more numbered boulders, marking former house sites, along the next half-mile of trail.

6.6   At a tree marked by double orange blazes, turn LEFT, and after ten yards cross a culvert marked by a metal drainpipe. Continue on this trail, following the double orange blazes.

6.8   You reach Whale's Jaw, marked by a post numbered 17.

This huge chunk of split granite, vaguely shaped like a whale's jaw

One of Dogtown's carved boulders

protruding up through the hill, is a popular destination for hikers and picnickers. If you are agile enough, climb to the top for a good view of the surrounding coastline.

After viewing Whale's Jaw, continue STRAIGHT, following the trail marked by double orange blazes.

7.3   At a T intersection marked by a post numbered 18, turn RIGHT.

7.6   Pass through a metal gate and turn LEFT onto a dirt road (Squam Road). Continue on this road, which soon turns to pavement.

8.2   At the end of the road, turn RIGHT (MA 127).
        If you prefer to return to the start of the ride by trail instead of pavement, take your first right onto Summit Avenue. At the end of Summit Avenue, Rockport Town Forest trails lead back into Dogtown and eventually connect with the trails you came out on. The way is not clearly marked, however, so be prepared to do some exploring.

8.6   At an intersection, turn RIGHT to stay on MA 127.
        If you turn left at this intersection onto Main Street, in a half-mile you

will reach Bearskin Neck, Rockport's artist colony/fishing village/ tourist attraction. Head down this way if you want to see the town or get a bite to eat before heading back.

10.8   You are back at the corner of MA 127 and Pond Street, where the tour began.

Bicycle Service

Giles of Gloucester, 32-38 Maplewood Street, Gloucester (508-283-3603). Sales, service, rentals.

Palazola's Sporting Goods, 96 Main Street, Gloucester (508-283-9180). Sales, service.

Great Brook Farm State Park

Distance: 5.0 miles
Terrain: Flat to rolling dirt path and forest trail
Difficulty: Easy
Map: Great Brook Farm State Park (available at parking area)

Great Brook Farm State Park is a unique facility in the Massachusetts state forest system. The park itself, a 935-acre forest reservation located in the town of Carlisle, is similar to many other state parks. What makes it distinctive is that incorporated into the park is a modern, productive, working dairy farm. Ninety acres of park land, barns and a farmhouse have been leased to a couple who maintain a herd of dairy cows, using the land to graze the herd and to grow corn and hay for feed. The farm and the park are well integrated, with trails that run along cornfields and cow pastures and give visitors a close-up view of the farm's workings.

The farm at Great Brook continues a tradition of agriculture on land that has been cultivated for hundreds of years. The original inhabitants of Carlisle, the now-extinct Massachuset Indians, hunted, fished and farmed in the area long before white settlers arrived. Since they did not have the use of saws, the Massachusets cleared the land by burning and used the resultant open fields to raise corn, beans and squash. When the English arrived in the 1630's, they purchased land from the Indians and parceled it out to the settling families. Although there was some industry in Carlisle, it was primarily an agricultural town, and the Great Brook property was farmed by a number of different families throughout the eighteenth and nineteenth centuries. In 1940, Farnham Smith bought eight acres of land on which the present Great Brook Farm buildings are located, and over the next 15 years he acquired eight adjoining farms and consolidated them into a single 875-acre spread. Smith's dairy cows, known as Fernhame Holsteins, won numerous prizes and had a major impact on the New England dairy industry. Smith sold his farm to the state in 1974, which developed it into the Great Brook Farm State Park. In order to keep the farming tradition on the land alive, in 1987 the state leased a portion of the park to the present managers, who have been running a successful dairy farm ever since.

Great Brook Farm is built around a farmhouse constructed in 1781 by Captain Timothy Ames, a veteran of the Battle of Bunker Hill. In addition to the house itself, there are barns, silos and a feeding area for

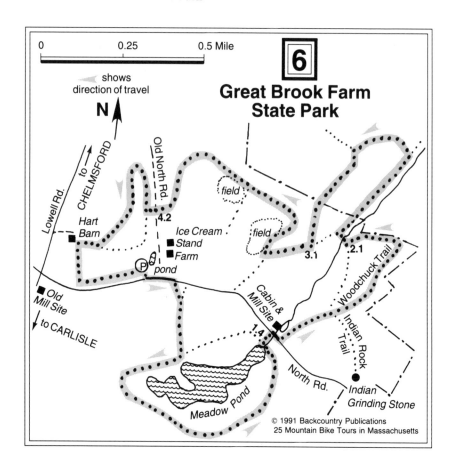

the cows as well as fields nearby which are used for pasture and field crops. Attached to the main barn is an ice cream stand, one end of which has a glass wall that lets the cows in the barn get a close look at humans during feeding time. If you would like to learn more about the workings of the farm, you can take one of the guided tours offered by the park service. Call the state park headquarters (number given below) to find out when tours are scheduled.

Because Great Brook is a working farm, certain areas are off-limits to visitors, including most of the farm buildings, active fields and pastures. Many of the trails in the park run along the perimeter of the fields, so please keep at least 15 feet away from the edge of these fields at all times. Off-limit areas are clearly marked, and the pastures are enclosed by electric fences to keep visitors away from the cows.

The park is much used by horseback riders, so it is important to slow down around corners or whenever you don't have a clear view of the trail ahead. Remember that when approaching a horse from the front, a mountain biker should stop and move off the trail until the horse passes. When approaching a horse from behind, call ahead to the rider from a safe distance to make sure it's okay to pass.

This ride circles the park along the bridle paths, forest trails and grassy paths that edge the pastures and fields. The flat, smooth trails and only occasional hills provide easy riding, making it ideal for beginners, or a perfect place to take the family mountain biking on a sunny Sunday afternoon.

To Get There: From MA 128 (I-95) take exit 31B for MA 4, MA 225, Bedford. Follow MA 225 West for 7.1 miles to the traffic circle in Carlisle center, then turn right onto Lowell Road, following the sign marked Chelmsford, 5. Follow Lowell Road for 1.8 miles, then turn right onto North Road at the sign for Great Brook Farm State Park. Follow North Road for 0.4 mile, then turn left at the sign for Great Brook Farm State Park into a parking lot beside a pond and farm buildings.

The Ride

0.0   The ride begins from the parking lot next to the farm buildings. From the parking lot, turn LEFT onto the paved road (Lowell Road).

0.1   At a sign marked The Meadows, Public Use Area, Pine Point Loop, turn RIGHT through an opening in a wooden fence onto a narrow dirt path which runs across an open field. After 100 yards, turn RIGHT onto a wide dirt path. Continue on this path, which is marked by blue triangles painted on the trees, as it winds through open fields and forest on its way around a number of small ponds and marshes.

> If you are looking for a place to spread out your lunch, there are several picnic tables scattered through the woods along this section of the trail.

1.4   As you approach a metal gate by a paved road, bear LEFT on a narrow dirt path. After 50 yards, cross a small wooden bridge over a stream into the parking lot for the canoe launching area. From this parking lot, turn RIGHT onto the paved road (North Road) and then immediately LEFT onto a dirt path marked by a No Parking sign. After 15 yards, go through a metal gate and continue STRAIGHT on this path.

1.5   You pass by a wooden cabin on the left.

> This cabin sits at the edge of Meadow Brook, the "great brook" for which the farm and the park were named. Like many other streams in New England, Meadow Brook was favored by the early settlers for the convenience and prosperity its water power offered, and the remains of a dam built to power grist-, hoop- and sawmills in the early 1700's are still visible. The village that grew up around these

mills had so many buildings it was referred to as "the city" by local residents. Today, there is almost no trace of the village, but if you wander around the woods near the dam's remains, you might find the cellar holes of some of the old mill buildings.

A mile or so upstream from this point, at the corner of Lowell Road and North Street, you can see the remains of another old dam, the site of a fulling mill built in 1691 and one of the first of its kind in

North America. Fulling was the final step in the long and tedious process of preparing wool cloth. To make a wool garment, the early settlers first had to raise the sheep and then shear them. The raw wool was then combed, washed, carded and spun into yarn, and the yarn dyed and woven into cloth. Because it was loosely woven, this homemade cloth was not good for keeping out the winter winds, so to tighten it, the cloth was fulled, a process that involved washing and beating the material with wooden paddles then treating it with Fuller's Earth, a clay imported from England, to remove dirt and animal grease. The wool was then compressed in water to shrink it into a tighter weave, after which it was smoothed, stretched, and dried, then the nap finished. Although the fulling process could be done by hand, the convenience offered by the water-powered fulling mill must have been greatly appreciated by the settlers.

With the growth of the textile industry in the nineteenth century, fulling mills became obsolete and this site was converted to other uses. In the late 1800's, the former fulling mill was used as a hoopmill, one of four located in the town of Carlisle. In a hoopmill, birch logs were sawed into long and flexible slats of wood, or hoops, that were used for packaging. Carlisle's hoopmills mostly supplied Somerville's meatpacking plants and Florida orange growers. The hoop business thrived in Carlisle until the early 1900's, when wire and other forms of metal packaging replaced the use of birch hoops.

1.6 At a fork, bear RIGHT (Woodchuck Trail).

Ten yards after this fork, a sign on the right marks the Indian Rock Path, a hardly visible path leading off to the right through the woods. If you follow this path, in approximately 0.3 mile you come to the Indian Grindstone, a rock with its top hollowed out from its use by Indians for grinding corn. The grindstone is clearly marked by a wooden sign on the left side of the trail.

1.8 At a fork marked by the remains of some old stone walls, bear LEFT. Continue on this trail through the woods, along a narrow clearing, and then back into the woods.

2.1 At a fork, bear RIGHT, and after 70 yards cross a wooden bridge over a stream. Immediately after crossing the bridge, turn RIGHT onto a narrow trail running parallel to the stream. Continue on this trail, bearing RIGHT at successive forks to follow the trail as it runs along the left side of the stream.

2.5 As a house comes into view approximately 150 yards ahead, bear LEFT at a fork. Continue on this trail as it passes just behind a number of houses on your right and then curves back around to the left, away from the houses.

2.8 At a T intersection, turn LEFT. Continue on this trail, passing by back-yards on the right, one of which contains a small horse farm.

3.0 At a fork at the top of a small, steep gully, bear RIGHT down the gully and up the other side.

3.1 You emerge from the woods at a clearing where a number of trails converge, with a narrow gas-pipeline running left to right and an open field directly ahead. Continue STRAIGHT on a mown grass path that runs across the open field.

3.2 In the center of the field, turn RIGHT onto a mown grass path. After 100 yards, continue STRAIGHT on the path as it moves into the woods, passes through an opening in a stone wall and continues up a steep hill.

3.5 As you emerge into an open field bounded by an electric fence, with a view of the farm buildings ahead, turn RIGHT onto a grass path that runs along the field's edge. Continue on this path as it passes along the edge of successive fields.

3.9 At the corner of a field where a dirt track leads off to the left, continue STRAIGHT through a small stand of trees into another field. Continue following this path as it crosses this field, turns left through a stand of trees and then crosses another field.

4.2 Continue STRAIGHT across a dirt road (Old North Road) to the corner of an open field that has a view to the left of the pond at which you started. From the corner of this field, turn RIGHT on a path that follows along the woods parallel to the dirt road you just crossed.

4.3 At a fork, bear LEFT, and in 70 yards, as you emerge from the woods into an open field, turn LEFT. Continue on a mown grass path that runs along the edge of the woods and then bears left across an open field.

4.5 As you pass through a line of trees that marks the boundary between two fields, turn RIGHT at a T intersection.

4.6 Fifty yards before reaching a red barn (Hart Barn), turn LEFT onto a mown grass path that cuts across a field to the left. The beginning of this path may not be mown and can be difficult to see. Continue on this path as it curves to the left and runs along the outside edge of the field, just beside a paved road (North Road) on the right.

5.0 You are back at the parking lot by the farm buildings, where the tour began.

> While you enjoy a well-deserved, post-ride ice cream, you may want to have a closer look at the dairy farm. About 120 head of cattle are kept on the farm, although only 50 or so are milked at any one time; the others, young calves, pregnant females and older cows, are kept as dry stock. The cows are milked by a vacuum-pumped,

gravity-fed pipeline that funnels the milk into a large tank where it is cooled and stored. Each cow must be milked twice a day, every day of the year. Every other day a milk truck comes by, collects the milk from the storage tank, then brings it to a processing plant where the milk is pasteurized, homogenized and bottled.

The fields around the farm are used in summer to grow the corn and hay that feed the cows year round. The hay is cut four times during the summer, and after cutting is chopped, compacted and stored in huge white plastic bags. Sealed inside these bags, the hay ferments into haylage, which makes up the bulk of the cows' diet. The same method is used to process the corn, which ferments into corn silage. Each bag holds 135 tons of feed, about 40 days' supply for the hungry herd.

Additional Information

Great Brook Farm State Park Headquarters, 841 Lowell Street, Carlisle, MA (508-369-6312).

Bicycle Service

Bedford Cycle and Fitness, 345 Great Road, Bedford (617-280-2453). Sales, service.

King Cycle, 198 Great Road, Bedford (617-275-2035). Sales, service.

Chelmsford Cyclery, 7 Summer Street, Chelmsford (508-256-1528). Sales, service, rentals.

Harold Parker State Forest

Distance: 9.6 miles
Terrain: Rolling dirt path, some forest trail and connecting pavement
Difficulty: Easy to moderate
Map: Harold Parker State Forest (available at forest headquarters and contact station)

At Harold Parker State Forest, the operative word on a mountain bike is *cruising*. Although you won't find many steep, narrow, twisting trails that challenge your limits as a rider, you will find miles of old forest roads, now wide dirt paths that seem to have been created just for cruising on a mountain bike. The forest is comprised of over 3,000 acres of woodlands and lakes located in the towns of Andover, North Andover and North Reading. The size of the forest, its location less than an hour from Boston and the 36 miles of trails that cross it make this area an ideal mountain-biking destination. It is also a popular family camping area, with 130 campsites, picnic facilities and ponds for fishing, swimming and boating.

The history of the Harold Parker State Forest begins as early as 7,000 B.C. Archaeological sites found in the forest evidence prehistoric tribes that lived and hunted in the Merrimack Valley. When the first white explorers arrived in the area, they were greeted by Indians of the Pennacook Confederacy. The Pennacook, who spoke Algonquian, lived in camps in the forest, planted corn and tobacco, and fished for salmon and alewives in the streams. In 1641, the first permanent white settlement was built, and shortly thereafter Chief Cutshamache sold the land comprising what is now Andover to the settlers for "six pounds of currency and a coat" and the right for Roger, a local Indian, to continue to plant corn and take alewives from the streams. The terms of this agreement, unfair as it may seem, are commemorated in the Andover town seal.

As the town of Andover and its neighboring communities grew through the eighteenth and nineteenth centuries, the forest was used as a source of lumber and firewood, its land cleared for farming, mills constructed along its rivers, and granite and soapstone mined from its quarries. In 1915, when the first 1,000 acres of the state forest were acquired in Andover, the land was not much to look at. Used extensively for lumbering and devastated by a fire in 1895, the state forest at that point was "a dry, bushy area filled with oak stump sprouts and suffering from too much runoff of water." The forest stayed that way until 1933, when the Civilian Conservation Corps (CCC) appeared on the scene. This was an organization created in 1933 by President Roosevelt for the dual purpose of providing jobs for the unemployed and promoting the cause of conservation. At Harold Parker, two CCC camps were established. Crews of workers built roads and campsites, replanted the forest and dug ponds for fishing and swimming. Thanks to the efforts of the CCC, the forest today is a place of beauty and vitality and a popular site for hikers, campers, boaters, swimmers and bikers.

To Get There: From I-93 take exit 40 for MA 62, North Reading, Wilmington. Follow MA 62 East for 4.2 miles, then turn left onto Haverhill Street. Follow Haverhill Street for 2.7 miles, then turn left into the state forest at a small brown building, which is the state forest contact station. Park in the lot immediately on the left after entering the state forest.

The Ride

0.0 The ride begins at the contact station. From the contact station, turn LEFT onto Haverhill Street.

0.3 Turn LEFT onto Harold Parker Road.

1.3 At a metal gate, turn RIGHT onto a dirt path. Continue on this path as it winds past two ponds and past paths intersecting from the left.

2.0 Turn RIGHT on a dirt path that angles back sharply to the right.

2.5 As the path turns sharply to the right, turn LEFT onto a narrow trail marked by two white paint blazes. Watch closely for this trail, as it is easy to miss. Follow this trail as it runs down a hill and alongside a rocky stream, and then crosses the stream on a wooden bridge and continues through the woods.

The dark, dank, boulder-choked stream crossed on this section of trail is what remains of the Skug River, once a fast-flowing waterway that powered a number of mills in this area. One, a sawmill, was owned by William Jenkins, a prominent member of the Jenkins family that lived on the border of the forest. He had inherited the mill from his grandfather, along with a soapstone quarry located nearby. In 1834, Jenkins formed a partnership to mine soapstone from this quarry and carve it at his mill. The soapstone, which is soft and easily cut, was sold for use in everything from buildings to tombstones to small, carved blocks that were heated and carried to church to keep hands warm during long services. Jenkins' soapstone business boomed, until the treasurer of the company embezzled the profits and took off for parts unknown.

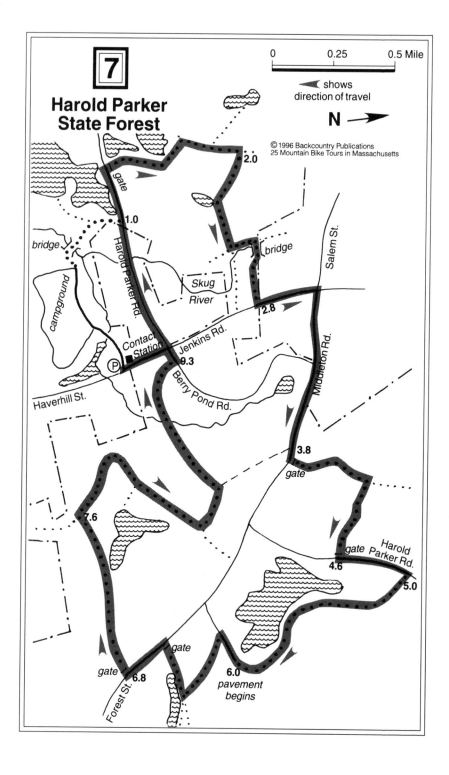

7

**Harold Parker
State Forest**

0   0.25   0.5 Mile

shows
direction of travel

N

© 1996 Backcountry Publications
25 Mountain Bike Tours in Massachusetts

2.0

gate

1.0

bridge

bridge

Salem St.

campground

Harold Parker Rd.

Skug
River

2.8

Contact
Station

Jenkins Rd.

P

9.3

Berry Pond Rd.

Middleton Rd.

Haverhill St.

3.8

gate

7.6

gate

Harold
Parker Rd.

4.6

5.0

gate

6.8

gate

6.0
pavement
begins

Forest St.

2.7   Just after passing a large, freestanding boulder on your left, follow the trail as it descends steeply into a gully and climbs out the other side into a clearing that leads to a paved road. You may have to carry your bike along this section of trail.

2.8   Turn LEFT onto the paved road (Jenkins Road).

In the mid-1800's, the area around the Harold Parker State Forest became famous as a center of the local abolitionist movement. Several of the houses near the forest were stops along the Underground Railroad, and Frederick Douglass, Harriet Beecher Stowe and William Lloyd Garrison were known to have visited families living there. In addition to being a businessman, William Jenkins, after whom the road you are now on was named, was also known as an outspoken, obstinate, well-intentioned idealist and a leader of the abolitionist movement. Elected state representative in 1854 on the Know-Nothing Party ticket, he used every opportunity to voice his liberal, antislavery views. His house was well known as a station on the Underground Railroad which transported fugitive slaves to safety in Canada. Arriving under cover of darkness, these slaves were hidden in the house until they could be transported to their next destination in New Hampshire. The house still stands at 89 Jenkins Road, and recent renovations revealed a secret room hidden underneath the attic floorboards.

3.1   Turn RIGHT on a paved road (Middleton Road), following a sign for Harold Parker State Forest.

3.8   At a wire gate marked by a sign saying Recreational Trail, Vehicles Prohibited, turn LEFT onto a dirt path.

4.2   At a small clearing, bear RIGHT onto a broad dirt path.

4.6   At the end of the path, pass through a wire gate and turn LEFT onto a paved road (Harold Parker Road).

5.0   At a wire gate marked by a sign saying Recreational Trail, Vehicles Prohibited, turn RIGHT onto a dirt path.

6.0   Continue STRAIGHT as the dirt road turns to pavement.

6.2   Seventy-five yards before reaching a metal gate, turn LEFT onto a dirt path that angles back sharply to the left.

6.5   As you reach the corner of a pond, bear RIGHT on a path that leads toward the road.

6.6   As you reach the road, pass through a wire gate and turn LEFT (Forest Street).

6.8   At a wire gate marked by a sign saying Recreational Trail, Vehicles Prohibited, turn RIGHT onto a dirt path.

7.6 At a T intersection, turn RIGHT. Continue on this path, staying to the left at subsequent forks.

9.3 Pass through a gate into a dirt parking lot. At the end of the parking lot, turn LEFT onto a paved road (Berry Pond Road) and after 100 yards, turn LEFT again (Haverhill Street).

9.6 You are back at the contact station, where the tour began.

Additional Information
Harold Parker State Forest Headquarters, 1951 N. Turnpike Road, N. Andover, MA (508-686-3391).

Bicycle Service
Cycle Shop, 134 Park Street, North Reading (508-664-6420). Sales, service.
Hope's Bicycle and Lawn Mower Sales and Service, 293 Hillside Road, North Andover (508-687-0611). Sales, service.
Dunn's Bike Shop, 16 Gould Street, Reading (508-944-9221). Sales, service.

Plum Island

Distance: 21.6 miles
Terrain: Flat; pavement and rough dirt road
Difficulty: Easy
Map: Parker River National Wildlife Refuge (available at refuge entrance); USGS 7.5′ × 15′ Newburyport; USGS 7.5′ × 15′ Ipswich

Unlike most mountain bike rides, the pleasure of riding at Plum Island is not so much in the voyage as in the destination. The roads covered on this tour—flat pavement and dirt—will not provide many thrills or challenges. They will, however, lead you to one of the best places for viewing wildlife in eastern Massachusetts as well as give you access to seven miles of secluded, dune-backed barrier beach, unquestionably the most pristine section of seashore north of Cape Cod. While you can travel these same roads by car, you will appreciate them more by bike. Instead of traveling as an observer, watching the scenery roll by your car window as if it were on a TV screen, on a bike you will become part of the landscape, moving along at just the right pace to allow you to take in the details and nuances of this remarkably vital environment.

As you ride along Plum Island, you will recognize that you are not the first person to admire this narrow strip of coastline. Its beaches, marshes and dunes were first visited by the Agawam Indians, who spent summers there planting and fishing; the harsh winters kept them from establishing permanent camps. Middens, piles of discarded clam shells found among the dunes, give evidence of the Indians' presence and of their taste for fresh shellfish. The Agawam had the island to themselves until the 1630's, when the first white settlers arrived in the Newburyport area. These settlers found Plum Island to be heavily wooded with tall, straight pine trees and covered with an abundance of beach plums, for which the island was named.

The pristine state in which the settlers found the island did not last long. As the settlements in the area grew, the pine was cut for lumber and firewood, and the resulting open land was used for grazing livestock. It was not long before the grazing began to take its toll on the dunes and marshes, and by 1739, it had been made illegal. As vegetation disappeared, the residents realized that without a plant cover they would soon have no beach left. After grazing stopped, the island was used for the harvesting of salt marsh hay. Through the mid-1800's, hay was mown in the marshes and piled on round straddles to keep it above the water until it could be gathered. Used as feed for animals, salt marsh hay was smuggled into Boston during the Revolution to sustain livestock when the British blockaded Boston Harbor.

After salt marsh hay, the next "crop" to be harvested on the island was tourists. In 1806 a bridge was built from the mainland, and by 1807 one of the first summer hotels in the United States had been constructed there. Development of the island continued until the 1930's, when the Massachusetts Audubon Society acquired 1,600 acres on the south end to be used as a bird sanctuary. In 1942 the U.S. Fish and Wildlife Service incorporated this land as well as an additional 3,000 acres into the Parker River National Wildlife Sanctuary. The refuge presently covers the southern two-thirds of the island, while the northern third of the island has been further developed with houses and cottages.

Plum Island as a whole provides a textbook case of "what is" and "what could have been" on the Massachusetts coast. The northern third of the island, packed with ramshackle cottages built to the edge of the sand and interspersed with beach shops and seafood restaurants, is a prime example of the unregulated development typical of much of the coastline. The southern two-thirds of the island has been protected from development by the Parker River NWR. On one side of the refuge is the beach—wild and desolate. Backing the beach is an undulating ribbon of dunes, and behind them are flat plains of marsh, a teeming preserve of birds and wildlife. The entire coastline was once like this; now only a small piece remains untouched.

Although the southern end of the island may be a paradise, it has its price in the form of greenhead flies, which breed profusely in the nearby marshes. From mid-July to the end of August, they make visiting the beach an excruciating experience and one best avoided. Because of the flies, this ride is best done in spring or fall, when temperatures are cooler and the bugs out of the picture. If you do decide to visit during summer, call ahead to see if the greenheads are out. Also, be forewarned that the number of people allowed in the refuge is strictly controlled, and the quota is usually reached by 8:30 or 9:00 a.m. on summer weekends. Once capacity is reached, the refuge is closed to visitors, whether on car, foot or bicycle, until 3:00 p.m. If you want to beat the crowds and get into the refuge before it is filled, you might wish to drive there directly, skipping that part of the ride running through downtown Newburyport. Doing so will shorten the total distance of the ride by 8.2 miles. A better alternative is to wait and visit the refuge after 3:00 p.m. when the gates are opened again. You can stay until the refuge closes one-half hour after sunset, which allows plenty of time to relax and explore.

Although mountain biking is allowed on the dirt road that runs through the center of the refuge, it is not allowed on any other part, including the beach and nature trails, in order to protect the fragile

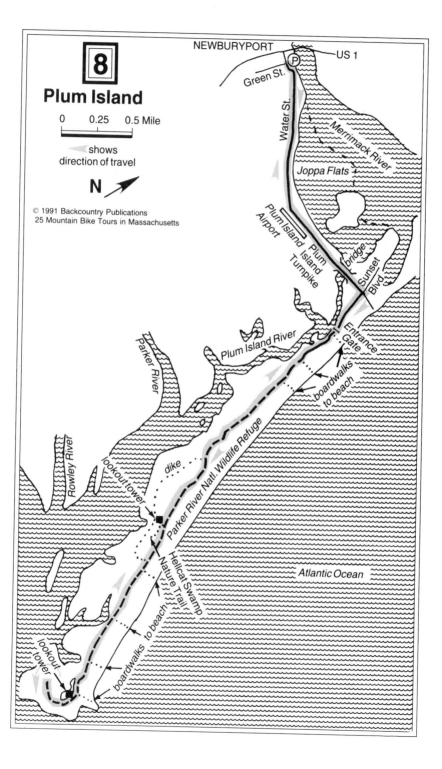

NEWBURYPORT

US 1

Green St.

8

Plum Island

0   0.25   0.5 Mile

shows
direction of travel

N

© 1991 Backcountry Publications
25 Mountain Bike Tours in Massachusetts

Water St.

Merrimack River

Joppa Flats

Plum Island
Airport

Plum Island
Turnpike

bridge

Sunset
Blvd

Entrance
Gate

boardwalks
to beach

Plum Island River

Parker River

lookout tower

dike

Parker River Natl. Wildlife Refuge

Rowley River

Atlantic Ocean

Hellcat Swamp
Nature Trail

boardwalks to beach

lookout
tower

ecosystem of the island. There are seven parking lots along the road that runs down the island, most of which have boardwalks to the beach. However, some of these lots may be closed and access to the beach restricted. Please respect these restrictions as well as any others that may be in force when you visit.

To Get There: From I-95, take exit 56 for Scotland Road, Newbury, West Newbury. Turn right on Scotland Road toward Newburyport. Follow Scotland Road for 3.2 miles, then turn right at a stop sign, following the sign for downtown Newburyport. After 0.2 mile, turn left at a traffic light, again following the sign for downtown Newburyport, and after 0.4 mile, bear right, still following the sign for downtown Newburyport. After 200 yards, turn right at a stop sign. After 0.2 mile, turn left into a parking lot next to Davis Auto Electric, at the intersection of Green and Water Streets. This lot has free all-day parking.

The Ride

0.0   Exit the parking lot and turn LEFT onto Water Street. Continue on Water Street as it winds through the center of Newburyport, then runs alongside the Merrimack River. Stay on Water Street as it becomes the Plum Island Turnpike and passes a small airport on the right.

The water (or mud, depending on the tide) to your left as you ride out of Newburyport is not the ocean but the Merrimack River, which reaches the Atlantic at the north end of Plum Island. The airport on the right is home to a number of ultralight airplanes, and on a fair day you can usually see one or two of these motorized hang gliders buzzing overhead as you ride by.

3.5   After crossing a bridge onto Plum Island, turn RIGHT on Sunset Boulevard, following the sign for Parker River National Wildlife Refuge.

4.1   You reach the Parker River National Wildlife Refuge entrance. Pass through the gate and continue STRAIGHT on the paved road that runs through the refuge. In approximately one mile, the pavement ends and the road turns to rough dirt.

If you would like to explore the beach, stop at one of the parking lots along the road, most of which have boardwalks running through the dunes to the ocean. The boardwalks were installed to protect the fragile dunes, so do not wander off them. If your conscience is not strong enough to keep you on the boardwalks, the poison ivy that grows abundantly in this area should be.

If you visit the beach on a day when the wind is blowing onshore, you will see the dangerous surf that has long made Plum Island a mariner's graveyard. Scores of ships have sunk off the island, with over 100 serious disasters since 1874. The number of

Plum Island

wrecks here and elsewhere along the U.S. coastline provided the impetus for the creation of the United States Life Saving Service in 1871, and the establishment of the first life-saving station on Plum Island in 1874. The Life Saving Service, a predecessor of the Coast Guard, set up life-saving stations along the coast and equipped them with emergency provisions, surf boats, life lines and special rescue equipment. The stations were manned by highly trained crews that patrolled the beach 24 hours a day, even in the worst weather, looking for ships in trouble. The service was responsible for saving hundreds of lives and existed until 1915 when it was merged into the newly formed U.S. Coast Guard.

7.9   On your right is a parking area for the Hellcat Swamp Nature Trail.
The Hellcat Swamp Nature Trail takes you on a walk through Plum Island's five different ecosystems: freshwater marsh, saltwater marsh, back dunes, primary dunes and beach. The salt and freshwater marshes are kept separate by a man-made dike that runs between them, and each supports a unique mix of wildlife. The marshes are located along a major bird migration path, and over 300 species of birds have been identified in the refuge. If you would like to follow this trail, please do so on foot, not on bicycle.

10.6 At the end of the road, turn RIGHT onto a sandy road that leads to a beach.

10.8 You reach the south end of Plum Island.
From the beach at this end you can look directly across Ipswich Bay to Crane Beach and Castle Hill. For an even better view, climb up the observation tower located nearby to survey the entire refuge and surrounding coastline.

After visiting the beach, return down the refuge road the way you came.

17.5 After exiting the refuge, turn LEFT onto the Plum Island Turnpike. Continue the way you came, following the Plum Island Turnpike as it becomes Water Street and leads into downtown Newburyport.

21.6 You reach the parking lot where the tour began.

Additional Information
Parker River National Wildlife Refuge, Plum Island, Newburyport, MA (508-465-5753). Open half hour before sunrise to half hour after sunset. Admission, bicycles $1.00, cars $5.00.

Bicycle Service
Life Sports, Fort Plaza Shopping Center, Newburyport (508-465-0011). Sales, service.

Ravenswood Park

Distance: 4.8 miles
Terrain: Rolling forest trail and gravel road
Difficulty: Easy to moderate
Map: USGS 7.5′ × 15′ Gloucester

Ravenswood Park is evidence that good things, even places to mountain bike, come in small packages. Ravenswood is a compact, largely untarnished jewel of a park, set just inland from the rocky shores of Cape Ann in Gloucester. The gravel roads and trails running throughout the park's 500 acres do not offer any epic adventures in vast, untamed backcountry, but will give you a few hours of some of the most enjoyable and picturesque riding north of Boston.

Ravenswood Park was created through the philanthropy of Samuel E. Sawyer, a Gloucester native who made his fortune in the Boston business world. He retained a love for his birthplace, returning every summer and buying up woodlots. Sawyer directed in his will that after his death (in 1882) a board of trustees be established to preserve the land he had amassed and develop it as a park "with driveways and pleasant rural walks." If Sawyer could see the park now, he would surely be happy that his wishes were carried out as he envisioned them. The park is lush, green and quiet, traversed by perfectly landscaped paths that flaunt its oak, pine, birch and hemlock forests, wind through its magnolia-filled swamps and snake down its granite-covered hillsides.

The well-maintained roads and trails in Ravenswood make it an ideal place for beginning mountain bikers to venture off-road. The wide gravel roads that run through the center of the park provide easy riding and a good surface for someone new to off-road riding to start out on, allowing one to get used to the feel of the bike. After warming up on the roads, riders can move on to the narrower and more challenging trails that circle the park's perimeter. For an even better introduction, it is possible to take a guided mountain bike tour through Ravenswood, given by Velotours, a bike-touring company that offers mountain bike rides throughout New England.

In order to cover the widest variety of terrain, this ride runs in two concentric loops through the park: the first is on the gravel roads that go through the interior of the park, and the second on the trails around the outside of the park. Because the tour doubles back on itself at some points, it is important to follow the written directions as well as the map.

To Get There: From MA 128 take exit 15 for School Street, Manchester, Essex. After exiting, turn right on School Street toward Manchester. Follow School Street for 0.5 mile, then turn left onto Lincoln Street at the sign for Magnolia, Gloucester. Follow Lincoln Street for 0.6 mile, then turn left onto MA 127 North. Follow MA 127 North for 4.1 miles, then turn left into the driveway next to the Ravenswood Community Chapel. The chapel can be difficult to see—it is a small, weathered clapboard building set back from the road. Park in the lot next to the chapel.

The Ride

0.0 Start on the gravel road (Valley Road to Old Salem Road) that leads from the parking lot into the park.

1.0 Stay on the gravel road (Old Salem Road to Evergreen Road) as it curves to the right at an intersection with a dirt track that continues straight into the woods.

> Just before this intersection, a plaque on a small boulder to the left marks the former site of a cabin occupied by Mason A. Walton, the Hermit of Gloucester. Walton moved to Gloucester from Boston in 1884 on the advice of a doctor who thought that the country air might relieve his aggravated dyspepsia, malignant catarrh, severe cough and sore lungs. Unable to find work in Gloucester because of his ill health, Walton moved into a tent in the woods. By his own account, after two weeks of life in the woods his cough was gone, and within two months the rest of his afflictions had also been cured. He eventually built a small cabin at this site and lived there for the next 18 years. Not a strict hermit, he occupied his time entertaining guests from Gloucester and making pets of the animals that lived in the woods around his cabin, including Satan, a raccoon, Bismarck, a red squirrel, and Wabbles, a song sparrow. He wrote about his encounters with these animals and his life in the woods, publishing a book in 1903 entitled *A Hermit's Wild Friends*.

1.4 At a T intersection with another gravel road (Quarry Road), turn LEFT. Stay on this gravel road as it curves to the right (Quarry Road to Ridge Road).

1.8 Turn LEFT as you rejoin the gravel road you started out on (Valley Road) heading back toward the parking lot. After a few hundred yards, turn RIGHT onto a dirt trail. This trail is easy to miss—look out for the small boulders that mark its entrance.

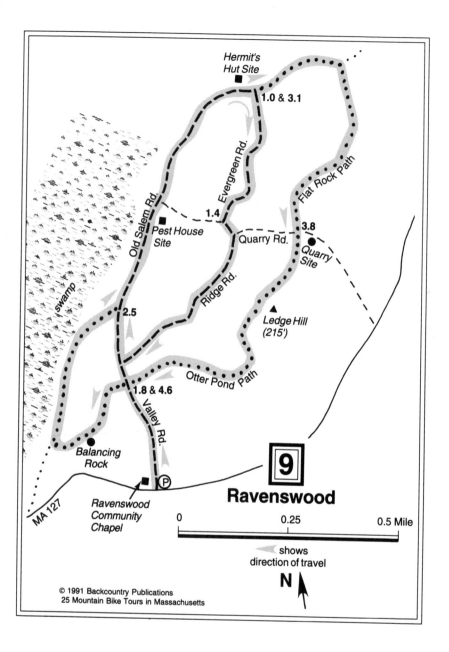

Hermit's
Hut Site

1.0 & 3.1

Evergreen Rd.

Flat Rock Path

Old Salem Rd.

1.4

Pest House
Site

Quarry Rd.

3.8

Quarry
Site

swamp

Ridge Rd.

▲ Ledge Hill
(215')

2.5

Otter Pond Path

1.8 & 4.6

Valley Rd.

● Balancing
Rock

Ⓟ

■ ▣

9

Ravenswood

MA 127

Ravenswood
Community
Chapel

| 0 | | 0.25 | | 0.5 Mile |

◄ shows
direction of travel

N ↑

© 1991 Backcountry Publications
25 Mountain Bike Tours in Massachusetts

2.0   You pass Balancing Rock, a huge boulder balanced on a flat slab of
granite.

> This boulder, dropped into its unlikely setting by the last glacier, is
> so perfectly balanced that it can be rocked when several people
> push against its side.

2.1 At an intersection with a wider path, turn RIGHT.

To your left as you ride along this trail is a swamp in which wild magnolia can be seen. This swamp is the northernmost point at which the plant grows, and the only place in Massachusetts where it is found. In earlier times, it was so plentiful in the area that it lent its name to the nearby village of Magnolia. In later years, however, magnolia became a popular decorative plant and was dug up to supply suburban gardens around the country. Eventually, what little was left in the area became protected by the creation of the park. If you don't mind a little mud, take one of the trails that lead into the swamp and look for the magnolia's fragrant white flowers in spring and its bright red berries in fall.

2.5 As you rejoin the gravel road (Old Salem Road), turn LEFT.

2.7 As a gravel road (Evergreen Road) enters from the right, you pass the former site of the pesthouse on the right.

The road you are now on, Old Salem Road, was the first land route between Gloucester and Salem, and was used until around 1800 when another road was laid closer to the coast. In its heyday, the road was a main thoroughfare and many houses were built along it. In 1777 the town of Gloucester built an isolation house for people with smallpox, and for a time the road was called Old Pest House Road. Today, nothing remains of the pesthouse but its name; the building is gone and its cellar hole filled in, leaving only a shallow depression taken over by the surrounding woods.

3.1 As the gravel road you followed earlier curves to the right, continue STRAIGHT onto a dirt track leading into the woods.

3.4 Just after crossing over a broad, smooth slab of granite, turn RIGHT onto a dirt trail (Flat Rock Path).

3.8 Cross over a gravel road (Quarry Road) and continue STRAIGHT on the trail.

Just to your left after crossing the road you can see the remains of an old quarry. Now a water-filled grotto, the smooth faces of granite and cylindrical grooves drilled into the rock reveal its former use.

After passing the quarry, the trail rapidly climbs to the top of Ledge Hill from where it then descends through a mass of granite boulders. As other trails intersect from the left and right, stay on the main trail (Otter Pond Path), which is lined on both sides by boulders.

4.6 At the end of the trail, turn LEFT onto the gravel road you started out on (Valley Road).

4.8 You are back at the parking lot where the tour began.

Additional Information

Velotours, 49 Front Street, Marblehead, MA 01945 (617-631-6184).

Bicycle Service

Giles of Gloucester, 32-38 Maplewood Street, Gloucester (508-283-3603). Sales, service, rentals.

Palazola's Sporting Goods, 96 Main Street, Gloucester (508-283-9180). Sales, service.

Borderland State Park

Distance: 7.7 miles
Terrain: Flat to rolling dirt and gravel road and forest trail with some connecting pavement
Difficulty: Easy to moderate
Map: Borderland State Park (available at visitor center); USGS 7.5′ × 15′ Brockton

Imagine riding a mountain bike through the grounds of an English country manor. You ride along smooth dirt roads, meandering lazily through open fields and lush groves of pine and beech. As you turn a corner, you come upon a group of summertime revelers spreading a sumptuous picnic on a wide, grassy lawn. Passing a cool, still pond, you wave to two small children drifting along lazily in a rowboat. In the distance, you can just hear the sound of hoofbeats as red-jacketed riders gallop their horses down wide bridle paths. Eventually, you arrive at the circular driveway of a vast stone mansion, where a liveried butler steadies your mountain bike as you dismount and escorts you into the drawing room for a glass of sherry.

Sound idyllic? Well, except for the butler and the sherry, you can find all of that and more at Borderland State Park. Borderland is a 1,200-acre reservation on the border (hence the name) of the towns of Sharon and Easton. The former estate of the Ames family, the well-manicured grounds of Borderland are more like a private garden than a state park. These grounds are a pleasure to explore by mountain bike: the interior of the park is crisscrossed by wide, flat dirt roads that are perfect for slow, easy mountain bike rides, while the forest on the periphery of the estate is laced with narrower, rockier trails that offer more challenging riding.

Borderland State Park came into being through the munificence of the Ames family, a locally famous clan that dug its way to fame and fortune via the shovel industry. The first notable member of the family was John Ames (1738–1803), a blacksmith and major of the Revolution who forged guns and shovels for the Continental Army. John's son, Oliver (1779–1863) turned his father's trade into a thriving business. Moving into a factory in North Easton, he developed a lightweight shovel that was superior to any other then available, and business boomed. Carrying on in their father's footsteps, Oliver's sons, Oakes (1804–1873) and Oliver (1807–1877) carried the business through the California gold rush, the Australian gold rush, the development of the Northwest Territories and the Civil War, all events that caused the demand for shovels to skyrocket and gave the Ameses a virtual monopoly in the industry. After their success in the shovel industry the brothers moved into the development of railroads, where they proceeded to lose the family fortune and then build it back again. Oakes' son, Oliver (1831–1895) expanded the family's influence, starting off in the shovel business and then leaving it for politics, serving three terms as governor of Massachusetts.

Oliver's son, Oakes (1874–1950) grew up in a privileged atmosphere of wealth and power that allowed him to turn the family efforts away from business and toward scholarship, public service and philanthropy. Oakes Ames was a professor of economic botany at Harvard University, a leading authority on orchids and director of the Arnold Arboretum in Boston. In 1900, Oakes married Blanche Ames (1878–1969), unrelated to Oakes despite having the same last name. She was a creative and energetic woman who was known as an inventor, a writer, and an accomplished artist as well as a pioneer in women's rights and advocacy of birth control.

In 1903, Oakes and Blanche Ames moved from North Easton into a house on Mountain Street in the rural part of Easton and acquired the first piece of what eventually would become Borderland. They took their life in the country seriously, working actively at clearing fields, cutting firewood, raising vegetables and managing livestock. Over the years, they bought land from four adjoining farms and fashioned a country estate, the centerpiece of which was a grand mansion they built on the site of an old farm house. Upon the death of Blanche Ames in 1969, the property was left in trust to her grandchildren who donated it to the state to be preserved for future generations.

Today, Borderland State Park is a well-managed and well-used recreation area. Its roads and trails are popular with hikers and equestrians, its ponds are frequented by rowers and paddlers, and the Ames mansion is preserved as a historic site. Because the park is used by horseback riders, it is important to bike slowly and with care, remembering that horses have the right of way on the trail. When approaching a horse from the front, a mountain biker should stop and move off the trail

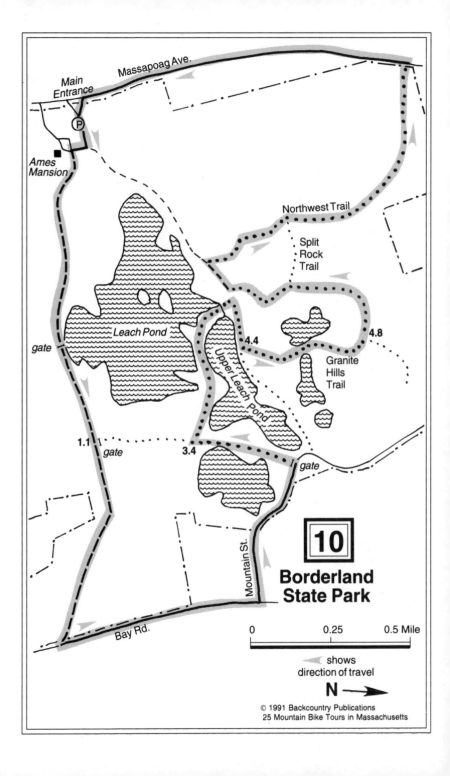

Main
Entrance

Massapoag Ave.

P

Ames
Mansion

Northwest Trail

Split
Rock
Trail

Leach Pond

Upper Leach Pond

gate

4.4

4.8

Granite
Hills
Trail

1.1

gate

3.4

gate

Mountain St.

Bay Rd.

10

Borderland
State Park

0   0.25   0.5 Mile

shows
direction of travel

N →

© 1991 Backcountry Publications
25 Mountain Bike Tours in Massachusetts

until the horse passes; when approaching a horse from behind, call ahead to the rider from a safe distance to make sure it's okay to pass.

To Get There: From MA 24 take exit 16B for MA 106 West, Mansfield. Follow MA 106 West for 5.0 miles, then turn right on Poquanticut Road at the sign for Borderland State Park. Follow Poquanticut Road for 1.3 miles, then turn left on Massapoag Avenue, following the sign for Borderland State Park. Follow Massapoag Avenue for 2.1 miles, then turn right at the sign for Borderland State Park into the parking lot.

The Ride

0.0 The ride begins from the parking lot. Start on the gravel road that runs from the parking lot into the park and across a wide lawn with the mansion on your right. At the end of the lawn, turn RIGHT toward the mansion, and after 75 yards, turn LEFT onto a gravel road toward the woods.

The Ames mansion was designed and built in 1910 by Oakes and Blanche Ames themselves. Blanche worked on the layout and floor plan of the house, while Oakes supervised the construction. Concerned about the possibility of fire, the Ameses fireproofed the house with a steel and concrete frame and sheathed it with rock cut from Borderland's stone walls. The house was designed in the style of an English country manor, with numerous windows and porches to create a sense of space and a feeling of communion with the outdoors. It was outfitted with all the latest conveniences of the time and was the first house in the area to have electricity and a garage for automobiles. Its many rooms include ten bedrooms, a library, trophy room, music room, studio and servants' quarters, all decorated with heirlooms inherited from both sides of the family. If you would like to see the interior of the house and learn more about the Ameses, visit Borderland on a Sunday afternoon when guided tours of the mansion are given.

0.4 On your right a placard marks the remains of a tree struck by lightning. Continue STRAIGHT on the gravel road.

0.8 Pass through a metal gate and continue STRAIGHT.

1.1 Continue STRAIGHT on the gravel road as you pass a white farmhouse and a gated path on the left.

1.8 The gravel road ends at a paved road. Turn LEFT onto this paved road (Bay Road).

2.5 Take your first LEFT onto a paved road (Mountain Street).

3.0 At a brown metal gate on the left side of the road, turn LEFT onto a dirt path.

3.4 As you reach an open field, the trail forks. Bear RIGHT on the trail that runs along the right edge of the field.

On this section of trail you pass between Leach Pond and Upper Leach Pond, both built by General Sheppard Leach around 1825 to supply water for an ironworks he constructed nearby.

4.0 Just after crossing a small stream, turn RIGHT at a T intersection.

The ride from this point on is along narrower, more difficult trails. If you would like to stay on the wide dirt roads, turn left at this intersection and follow the gravel road, which leads back to the parking lot. Or, turn left here and after 0.1 mile turn right onto the Northwest Trail, and skip ahead to the directions at mile 5.3.

4.4 Turn LEFT on the Granite Hills Trail, marked by a brown sign with white letters. After 50 yards, as you come to an open field, turn RIGHT and follow a barely visible path that circles along the right edge of the field.

4.6 Diagonally across from the point at which you entered the field, turn RIGHT onto a dirt trail that crosses a streambed.

4.8 Continue STRAIGHT on the lower loop of the Granite Hills Trail, indicated by a sign on the right marking its intersection with the upper loop.
To avoid erosion, be sure to use the footbridges to cross the streams along this section of trail.

5.0 Continue STRAIGHT on the Granite Hills Trail at a sign on the right marking its intersection with the Split Rock Trail. At a large, flat boulder, bear LEFT to stay on the trail.
This section of the Granite Hills Trail passes through a fascinating natural rock garden. Granite boulders of all sizes were dropped here by the last glacier, at some points spread so thickly that you can't see the ground for the granite. These boulders were picked up by the glacier from some unknown point to the north, perhaps from the summit of a New Hampshire mountain or the ledges of a Canadian cliff, and plunked down at this spot when the glacier melted.

5.2 At the end of the Granite Hills Trail, turn RIGHT onto a gravel road.

5.3 Turn RIGHT onto the Northwest Trail.

6.4 Bear LEFT at a fork.

6.6 At the end of the Northwest Trail, turn LEFT onto a paved road (Massapoag Road).

7.7 You are back at the parking lot, where the tour began.

Additional Information
Borderland State Park, Massapoag Avenue, North Easton, MA (508-238-6566).
Tours of the mansion, Sundays mid-April to mid-November, call for times.

Bicycle Service
Bike Shed of Easton, Inc., 285 Washington Street, Easton (508-238-2925). Sales, service.
Easton Bicycle, 447 Turnpike, Easton (508-238-7919). Sales, service.

F. Gilbert Hills State Forest

Distance: 12.2 miles
Terrain: Steeply rolling forest trail
Difficulty: Difficult
Map: F. Gilbert Hills State Forest (available at headquarters)

To ride a mountain bike well, you need to perfect the skills that allow you to master your local riding conditions. Since terrain in the U.S. varies from region to region, riders from different parts of the country must develop different types of expertise. In Colorado's Rockies, riders must be able to climb like a goat up steep grades through the thin air of the high peaks. Utah's slickrock canyons demand fluid bike handling and consummate ability in picking the right line across the rock. In California's redwood forests, mastering high-speed descents on smooth fire roads is a must. In New England, the challenges facing mountain bikers can be summed up in one word: rocks. More often than not, riding off-road in New England involves snaking through trees on a shoulder-width trail, twisting and balancing as you squeeze your way through a labyrinth of boulders waiting to grab the wheel of your bike and unexpectedly throw you headfirst into the woods.

The rockiness of New England's terrain originated approximately 15,000 years ago when the last glaciers receded from the Northeast, leaving a layer of crushed stone known as glacial till. The glacier was uneven in its work, in some places grinding the rock down to smooth sand, in others depositing it as vast boulders, and in still others uncovering the bedrock to lie in bare, exposed ridges. It is this glacial till, spread unevenly over rolling hillsides, that defines the typical boulder-strewn New England countryside, and thus the typical New England mountain bike trail. If you ride a mountain bike in New England for any length of time, you learn to love these granite-covered obstacle courses that hone your balance and push you to the limits of your bike-handling ability. And if you've learned to love trails like these, you'll enjoy riding at F. Gilbert Hills State Forest, 810 acres of dense woodland located in the town of Foxboro. The trail system at F. Gilbert Hills includes wide dirt roads and narrower bridle paths, but the primary reason to go there is for the miles of classic New England mountain biking: rocky, constricted trails that wind maze-like across the hilly contours of the glacier-shaped landscape.

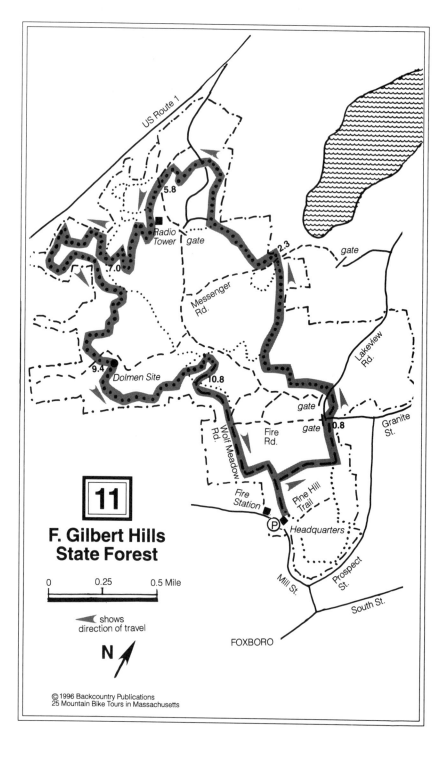

US Route 1

5.8

Radio Tower gate

7.0

2.3

gate

Messenger Rd.

Lakeview Rd.

9.4

Dolmen Site

10.8

gate

Fire Rd.

gate

Wolf Meadow Rd.

10.8

Granite St.

Fire Station

Pine Hill Trail

P

Headquarters

Prospect St.

Mill St.

South St.

FOXBORO

11

F. Gilbert Hills State Forest

0   0.25   0.5 Mile

◄ shows direction of travel

N ↗

© 1996 Backcountry Publications
25 Mountain Bike Tours in Massachusetts

If the attraction of these trails is not enough, F. Gilbert Hills offers a little mystery to go along with the riding. In one corner of the forest, amateur archaeologists have discovered a number of stone structures that are believed to date from prehistoric times. These include a dolmen, or stone altar, and a series of boulders precisely aligned with the earth's magnetic field. No one knows for certain who built these structures, when they were built, or what they were used for.

F. Gilbert Hills is one of the few state forests in Massachusetts to have trails that are specifically designated for mountain biking. This ride follows those trails, which form a loop around the perimeter of the forest. The route is easy to follow, as it is blazed at every junction by green triangular markers with a bicycle symbol.

The rocky terrain in the forest, along with constant short, steep uphills and downhills, conspire to make this ride a challenging one. In particular, the last few boulder-strewn miles of this route will have all but the most skilled mountain bikers pushing their bikes as much as riding them. Also, be aware that some of the trails covered on this ride are frequented by dirt bike and ATV riders. Fortunately, the noise made by these vehicles makes them easy to detect from a distance. If you hear one coming your way, stop riding and move well off the trail until it has passed.

To Get There: From I-95, take exit 8 for Foxboro, Sharon. At the end of the exit ramp, turn west on Mechanic Street toward Foxboro. Follow Mechanic Street for 2.3 miles to the rotary in Foxboro's center. Proceed two-thirds of the way around the rotary, then turn right onto South Street. Follow South Street for 1.5 miles, then turn right at the State Forest sign onto Mill Street. Follow Mill Street for 0.4 mile, then turn right at the F. Gilbert Hills State Forest sign into the parking lot.

The Ride

0.0 The ride begins from the state forest parking lot. Start on the dirt road (Wolf Meadow Road) that begins at the edge of the parking lot between the forest headquarters building and the fire station.

0.2 Turn RIGHT onto a wide dirt road. Note the green triangular bicycle marker pointing out this turn. You will be following these markers for the duration of the ride.

0.5 Bear LEFT as the Pine Hill Trail joins in from the right.

0.8 Continue STRAIGHT across a paved road.

0.9 Continue STRAIGHT across a paved road. The trail soon becomes narrow, steep, and rocky.

1.6   At a fork, bear RIGHT.

1.7   At a fork, bear RIGHT.

2.2   At a fork, bear RIGHT.

2.3   Bear RIGHT as you merge onto a dirt and gravel road (Messenger Road) joining in from the left.

2.5   Bear LEFT off the road onto a rocky trail that circles around a lake visible through the trees.

2.8   At a fork, bear LEFT as you continue around the lake.

3.2   At a fork, bear LEFT.

3.3   Bear LEFT as a trail joins in from the right.

4.3   As the trail you are on continues straight, turn sharply RIGHT onto a rocky, uphill trail.

4.4   As you come over the crest of a hill, bear RIGHT.

4.8   Turn LEFT onto a dirt and gravel road. In 100 feet, turn RIGHT off the road onto a trail. In 30 feet, continue STRAIGHT as you cross a wider trail.

5.2   Continue STRAIGHT as you cross an open area of rock.

5.3   At a fork, bear LEFT. In 100 feet, continue straight across a paved road.

5.5   The trail emerges from the woods and climbs up an open area of rock. At the top of this rock, make a U-turn to the right, and continue down the rock to rejoin the trail as it enters the woods.

If you stop here for a moment, you can hear the roar of traffic from nearby Route 1. Some two hundred years ago, you might instead have heard the clatter of stagecoaches along this same road, then called the Norfolk and Bristol Turnpike. Built in 1806 to improve travel between Boston and Providence, the turnpike was instrumental in introducing a new era of high-speed transportation, shortening by half what had been a ten-hour journey between the two cities.

The Norfolk and Bristol Turnpike was a toll road, with a gate in Foxboro at which travelers stopped and paid a tariff of 40¢ for coach and horses, 6¢ for horse and wagon, 5¢ for horse and rider, and herds at 2¢ per horse, 1¢ per cow and 10¢ per fifteen swine. A sec-

A prehistoric stone altar in Gilbert Hills State Forest

ond major highway also passed through Foxboro, and a hotel and two taverns sprung up at the crossroads to provide food and accommodations for road-weary travelers.

By 1825, four-hitch coaches were taking passengers from Boston to Providence on the turnpike for $3. The route was so popular that two rival companies started a fare war to compete for riders. The price was first dropped to $2.50 and then continued to drop as the competing companies tried to outdo one another. Then, one company got the idea of offering a free ride to the first passenger booked on a trip, and prices kept on falling until everyone was riding for free. Still not willing to give up, one company offered a free dinner at the end of the trip, and the other countered by offering a free dinner plus a free bottle of wine. For a short time, travelers were taking the free trip from Boston to Providence just to get the free meal at the end of the ride. Finally, the two companies realized that neither would survive long if the battle continued, and compromised on a set fare of $2.

The turnpike existed as a toll road until 1843, when it was opened to the public as a common highway and renamed Norfolk Street; in 1876 it was renamed Washington Street in honor of the Centennial. In 1931, the state took it over and it became the Route 1 of today.

5.7   Bear LEFT as you merge onto a wider trail coming in from the right.

5.8 Bear LEFT onto a wide dirt and gravel trail along a set of power lines.

5.9 One hundred yards before reaching a radio tower, turn RIGHT off the dirt and gravel trail onto a dirt trail.

6.0 Bear RIGHT. In 30 feet, bear LEFT.

7.0 Continue STRAIGHT across a four-way intersection.

8.4 Turn RIGHT onto a wider trail joining in from the left. In 100 yards, bear LEFT.

8.5 At a T intersection, turn LEFT.

8.7 Bear RIGHT.

9.2 Stay on the trail as it curves around to the left and two other trails join in from the right.

9.4 Continue STRAIGHT across a dirt road.
If you want to do some exploring, turn left on this dirt road. A short distance up on the right a clearing leads to a broad, flat outcropping of granite. Scattered about this clearing are a number of stone structures believed to be artifacts of a pre-Columbian civilization. The most intriguing is the dolmen, or altar stone, located on the left side of the clearing. It is a broad, flat slab of rock supported at three points by "legs" made of three or four flat stones. A bit farther down the clearing, toward the edge of the granite outcropping, are four huge boulders, equally spaced from each other and aligned precisely on a north-south axis. To the left of these boulders is a row of smaller rocks lying at an exact 15-degree angle to the larger rocks. In the forest around this outcropping, other stone structures have been found, including the remains of numerous domed enclosures and a second arrangement of boulders, again with four large ones aligned north-south and a row of four smaller rocks angled at 15 degrees to them.

While not as striking as Stonehenge, it's obvious that these rocks were not arranged by coincidence and that it must have taken a great deal of effort to move them into place. To date, however, there has been no professional archaeological investigation of the site and little is known of its origin. The only clues to these enigmatic relics have come from their comparison to a site in New Hampshire known as Mystery Hill, where a more extensive grouping of similar objects has been found. Because of the proximity and similarity of these two sites, it is possible that they are related. One of the more intriguing theories explaining these structures was put forth by William Goodwin, who visited the Foxboro site in the 1940s and later purchased and excavated much of Mystery Hill. After much research, Goodwin found that the artifacts at these two locations were similar to those at sites in Ireland, and concluded that they may have been built by the monks of Culdee in Ireland, who visited New England around the year 1000.

However, in 1975, a stone was found at Mystery Hill inscribed with Day 39, the date of the Celtic May Day celebration. Furthermore, carbon testing has dated objects from the same site at 1000 B.C. It is now believed that the stone structures at Mystery Hill, and by association those at Foxboro, are between 3,000 and 4,000 years old, possibly making them the oldest man-made constructions in North America. While intriguing, none of these theories are complete, and until the dolmen site is investigated more thoroughly its meaning will remain a mystery.

10.2 Turn RIGHT as a trail joins in from the left.

10.8 Turn RIGHT onto a dirt and gravel road (Wolf Meadow Road).

12.2 You are back at the state forest headquarters, where the tour began.

Additional Information

F. Gilbert Hills State Forest, Mill Street, Foxboro (508-543-5850).

Bicycle Service

Crossing Cycle, 282 Cottage Street, Franklin (508-528-1010). Sales, service.

Franklin Bicycle, 28 East Central Street, Franklin (508-520-2453). Sales, service.

Sirois Bicycle Shop, 893 Laundry Avenue, North Attleboro (508-695-6303). Sales, service.

Freetown-Fall River State Forest

Distance: 10.9 miles
Terrain: Flat to rolling dirt road and path, some connecting pavement
Difficulty: Easy to moderate
Map: Freetown-Fall River State Forest (available at forest headquarters); USGS
7.5′ × 15′ Somerset; USGS 7.5′ × 15′ Fall River

The sport of mountain biking appeals to a wide range of people, and just about everyone who owns a mountain bike has a different idea of what an ideal day on a bike entails. At one end of the spectrum are the casual riders whose idea of a perfect day combines easy peddling, scenic countryside and a long stop at an idyllic spot at which to spread the red-and-white-checked tablecloth and break out the Camembert and Cabernet. At the other end of the spectrum are the hardcore riders for whom a ride is not complete unless they come back bruised, battered and exhausted, having sweat up every hill, plummeted down every cliff and jumped every log within riding distance. With such a diverse lot of bikers, it's difficult to find a riding area with enough variety to keep all riders interested. Freetown-Fall River State Forest is one such place, as it offers some of the most diversified terrain in eastern Massachusetts: the trails range from gradually rolling dirt roads that gently welcome the efforts of first-time riders, to treacherous, twisting, motorcycle-carved trails that can cause even the toughest riders to land in the dirt.

Freetown-Fall River State Forest consists of over 5,400 acres twined by degraded dirt roads, bridle paths and motorcycle trails, including a marked 22-mile motorcycle loop which offers some of the most interesting, challenging and fun riding to be found anywhere. The motorcycle trails tend to be narrow, rolling and rutted, with steep climbs, precipitous drops and careening, banked corners. The toughest ones, over loose, rocky ground, are almost impossible to ride on a mountain bike, but others, especially those that wind through stands of widely spaced pine, give a smooth, rock-free roller coaster of a ride. If you are an intermediate rider or better, it's worth the trip to Freetown-Fall River just to take a spin on these trails.

Riding at Freetown-Fall River does require some caution. Although the motorcycle trails are fun to ride, because of the differences in speed at which a motorcycle and a mountain bike travel, sharing trails can be dangerous. If you hear a motorcycle coming, move well off the trail until it has passed. Motorcycle activity is highest on weekends, so you may want to avoid these trails then. If you do ride the motorcycle trails, you must be careful to do so in the right direction. All are one-way and marked with triangular signs displaying a picture of a motorcycle pointed in the direction of travel. Watch for these signs and make sure you are riding in the proper direction at all times.

Another aspect of riding at Freetown-Fall River that requires caution is hunting activity. One corner of the forest is a stocked game preserve, or Wildlife Management Area, and it's best to avoid this section during hunting season. Call ahead (number given below) to find out when hunting activity is high. If you do hit the trails during open season, the best way to avoid a case of mistaken identity is to wear something that no self-respecting deer would be caught dead in, such as a pair of fluorescent orange riding shorts.

One last bit of cautionary advice: Freetown-Fall River State Forest is vast, with a complicated trail system, and it's very easy to get lost in. Years of motorcycle activity have carved up the forest into a labyrinth of interweaving trails. Until you learn your way around, it's important to pay close attention to landmarks and to watch where you're going at all times. Because of the possibility of getting lost or hurt—and for your personal safety—the Freetown-Fall River State Forest is a place you should not ride in alone or after dusk.

This ride follows a broad loop that winds through a good portion of the forest's territory. It is designed to provide an overview of the trail system and therefore stays on the easier dirt roads. Once familiar with the forest, you can venture out on some of the more challenging trails which are pointed out along the way.

To Get There: From MA 24, take exit 10 for North Main Street, Assonet, Dighton. At the end of the exit ramp turn onto North Main Street following the sign for State Forest, Profile Rock. Follow North Main Street for 0.7 mile, then turn left on MA 79 North following the sign for State Forest, Profile Rock. In 0.1 mile, bear right at a fork onto Slab Bridge Road following the sign for State Forest, Profile Rock. Follow Slab Bridge Road for 1.9 miles, then turn right at the sign into the Fall River-Freetown State Forest. After entering the forest, in 70 yards turn left at Old Smokey's Shack onto an access road that leads to a parking lot by a picnic area.

The Ride

0.0   The ride begins from the parking lot by the picnic area. Start on the access road which leads out of the parking lot. At the end of the access road, in front of Old Smokey's Shack on the left, turn LEFT on a paved

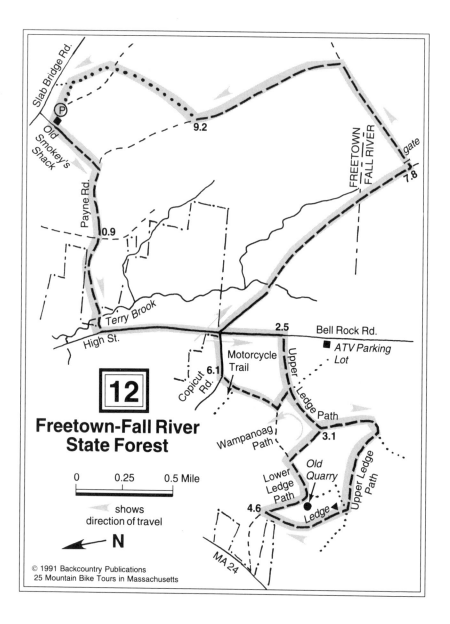

12

Freetown-Fall River State Forest

0   0.25   0.5 Mile

shows
direction of travel

N

© 1991 Backcountry Publications
25 Mountain Bike Tours in Massachusetts

road (Payne Road) which leads into the forest and soon turns to dirt. Along this section of the ride you will pass the start of the 22-mile motorcycle loop, which leads off to the left from Payne Road.

0.5 At a fork, bear RIGHT.

0.9 At a four-way intersection, continue STRAIGHT.

    As you ride along this road you pass over Terry Brook, one of the streams whose water power made Freetown prime real estate for the early settlers. When choosing a section of wilderness out of which to carve a settlement, the most important consideration for the colonists was access to a reliable spring that could provide year-round drinking water. If the land also happened to contain a stream that could be used to power a mill, all the better, as a mill could provide a much steadier source of income than farming alone. In Freetown, much of the land was crossed by fast-flowing streams. Although many of these were small, the difference in altitude between their source and their mouth meant that they had enough power to run numerous mills. At one point there were over 20 dams on the four streams that run within a few miles of the town's center. The water that collected behind each dam was used to power a mill, or sometimes two mills, one on either side of a stream. Many of these were sawmills, but there were also gristmills and ironworks, and mills for carding wool, making cotton batting, cutting shingles and forging nails. This added up to a great deal of industry, and therefore a great deal of prosperity for early Freetown.

The dam built on Terry Brook was probably first used to power a sawmill. In 1829, a cupola furnace was built there, which was operated until 1834. Subsequently, the mill was converted into a factory for constructing threshing machines, then a spooling mill, then a waste-cleaning mill. Finally, when the last mill burned down, the dam was removed to allow water to flow into the reservoir of a bleachery located downstream.

1.5 At the end of the dirt road, turn LEFT onto a paved road (High Street to Bell Rock Road).

2.5 Turn RIGHT on a wide dirt road (Upper Ledge Path) which runs through an open grove of pines. This road is approximately 0.3 mile before the ATV parking lot on the right—if you reach the parking lot, you've gone too far.

If you want to get on to the 22-mile motorcycle trail, continue straight to the ATV parking lot. From the corner of the parking lot, a sign points the way onto the trail.

2.9 At a four-way intersection, continue STRAIGHT.

3.1 At a fork, bear LEFT and continue on the dirt road (Upper Ledge Path) as it begins to climb.

3.9 At a four-way intersection with a dirt path, continue STRAIGHT.

4.1 At a four-way intersection with a dirt path, continue STRAIGHT.

4.2 You pass by a clearing on the right marked by a row of large boulders along the road.

Walk to the rock ledge at the far end of this clearing for a view across the forest from the top of a high cliff above an abandoned quarry.

After taking in the view, continue STRAIGHT on the dirt road as it begins to descend.

4.6   At a fork at the bottom of a hill, bear RIGHT (Lower Ledge Path).

4.8   At a three-way intersection beside an abandoned quarry on the right, turn LEFT on the dirt road farthest to the left, which runs down a small hill.

5.0   At a fork, bear RIGHT. Continue STRAIGHT as you merge with Upper Ledge Path, which comes in from the right.

5.6   At a four-way intersection, turn LEFT. In 0.1 mile, bear RIGHT onto a wide dirt path, and in 100 yards, bear RIGHT as a dirt road (Wampanoag Path) joins in from the left.

6.1   At the end of the dirt road, turn RIGHT onto a paved road (Copicut Road).
    About 0.1 mile before you reach the paved road there is a path that leads off to the left into the woods (it is the last left turn before reaching the paved road). This path is the beginning of one of the best and easiest sections of motorcycle trail in the forest—smooth and generally rock-free, with well banked corners. If you are interested in trying the motorcycle trails, this is a good one to start on.

6.3   At a four-way intersection marked by a sign on the right saying Wampanoag Indian Reservation, continue STRAIGHT across the intersection on a paved road that curves to the right and soon turns to dirt. Continue on this dirt road as it runs into the forest.

7.4   A sign on the left marks the border as you cross from Freetown into Fall River.

7.8   Turn LEFT on a wide dirt road and pass through a gate.

8.5   At an intersection marked by a lone tree in its center, turn LEFT on a wide dirt road.

9.2   Turn RIGHT onto a wide dirt path marked by a faded blue arrow painted on a tree on the right.

10.5   At a four-way intersection marked by a yellow triangular motorbike sign, continue STRAIGHT.

10.6   At a fork, bear RIGHT.

10.8   Thirty yards before reaching a paved road, turn LEFT on a dirt path.

10.9   You are back at the parking lot where the tour began.

Additional Information
Freetown-Fall River State Forest, Slab Bridge Road, Assonet, MA (508-644-5522).

Bicycle Service
Crosby's Cycle Company, 248 Tucker Street, Fall River (508-679-9366). Sales, service.
Paul's Schwinn Cyclery, 767 Pleasant Street, Fall River (508-674-0343). Sales, service.

Hale Reservation and Noanet Woodlands

Distance: 9.7 miles
Terrain: Forest trail and bridle path, rolling, with a few larger hills
Difficulty: Moderate
Map: Hale Reservation (available at Hale Reservation office); Noanet Woodlands (available at Noanet Woodlands ranger station); USGS 7.5′ × 15′ Norwood; USGS 7.5′ × 15′ Medfield

Hale Reservation and Noanet Woodlands are two separate but adjoining areas of conservation land in Westwood and Dover. Hale is a privately-owned reservation; Noanet Woodlands is a Trustees of Reservations property. Together they offer 1,600 acres of woodlands crossed by over 30 miles of well-marked trails and bridle paths. Although the two areas are next to each other, the terrain in each is different. Hale is forested with closely-spaced oaks and maples, with narrow trails running through dense underbrush. In Noanet Woodlands, wider paths run through open groves of pine. The trail systems for the two areas are connected, allowing you to ride from one to the other to cover maximum distance and variety of terrain.

Hale Reservation has the more interesting history. It exists as the legacy of one man's commitment to provide children with a place to learn about nature. Robert S. Hale, a devoted supporter of children's need for outdoor recreation, began to purchase land in 1918 for use as camps by the Boy Scouts and other youth groups. By 1927, Uncle Robert, as he was affectionately known by the Scouts, had acquired 1,200 contiguous acres in Dover and Westwood. He called the property Scoutland, and described its nature and purpose with these words:

> I should be pleased to have you use my land in Westwood for camping . . . and to do so with a feeling that it belongs to all. While the land is not very good for farming, it is more nearly wild country than any other place as near Boston with the woods extending unbroken for several miles. . . .

Over 30 outdoor recreation cabins were built on the land, and when Hale died in 1941 the reservation was named in his honor. Today, Hale Reservation is privately owned and run as a non-profit organization. It offers school and family programs as well as the largest day-camp program in the country, with 1,700 campers during the summer. Twenty miles of trails and ponds for boating, swimming and fishing make it a popular summer destination.

Well before Robert S. Hale was supporting the Scouts, however, archaic Indians living in what is now Dover were fashioning tools from stone quarried in the area 5,000 years ago, at about the same time the Egyptians were building pyramids along the Nile. Evidence of nine ancient rock quarries has been found in Hale Reservation, and archaeologists believe they were in use as early as 3,000 B.C. The quarries are found in places where veins of felsite emerge from the surrounding rock. The Indians broke off pieces of the exposed felsite to shape them into tools by splitting off small flakes, as indicated by the small chips of felsite that cover the ground around the quarries. They made spears, arrowheads and knives, examples of which can be seen in the reservation office.

The ride described below starts at the Hale Reservation office and runs halfway around the reservation's perimeter. It then joins the Noanet Woodlands trail system and rides a loop through Noanet, rejoining the Hale Reservation trails at the same point it left them, then continuing around the rest of the reservation. If you prefer a shorter ride, it is possible to skip the loop through Noanet Woodlands—the directions tell you how to do so. You may want to avoid riding in Hale Reservation when the summer camp is in session, as the trails can be crowded with campers. Also, the reservation is a popular place for hiking and horseback riding during summer weekends, so ride with caution during these times.

To Get There: From MA 128 (I-95) take exit 16B for MA 109 West, Westwood. Follow MA 109 West for 1.1 miles, then turn right onto Dover Road. In 0.3 mile, turn right on Carby Street, where you will see a sign for Hale Reservation. As you enter the reservation there is a small parking lot on the right, and the reservation office is on the left. There is also a larger parking lot (Cat Rock Parking Lot) 0.4 mile up the road.

The Ride

0.0 The ride begins at the Hale Reservation office. Proceed up the road (Carby Street) into the reservation. After 50 yards, turn RIGHT at a sign for Cat Rock and Wildflower Meadow onto a dirt trail (Storrow Pond Trail). This trail is marked by square metal blazes. It is important to keep an eye out for these blazes, as a number of trails cross the main trail. Although not always obvious, the blazes are there and will keep you on the right track.

0.1 Continue STRAIGHT across a gravel road. Just after crossing this road, bear LEFT at a fork, following the square metal blazes.

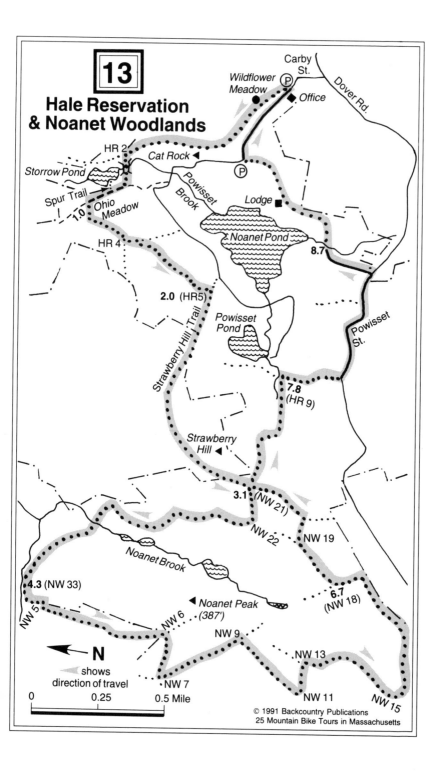

13

Hale Reservation & Noanet Woodlands

Wildflower Meadow

Carby St.

Dover Rd.

Office

HR 2

Cat Rock

Storrow Pond

Powisset Brook

Lodge

Spur Trail

Ohio Meadow

Noanet Pond

1.0

HR 4

8.7

2.0 (HR5)

Strawberry Hill Trail

Powisset Pond

Powisset St.

7.8 (HR 9)

Strawberry Hill

3.1 (NW 21)

NW 22

NW 19

Noanet Brook

4.3 (NW 33)

6.7 (NW 18)

NW 5

NW 6

Noanet Peak (387')

NW 9

NW 13

N

shows direction of travel

NW 7

NW 11

NW 15

| 0 | 0.25 | 0.5 Mile |

© 1991 Backcountry Publications
25 Mountain Bike Tours in Massachusetts

0.5 Pass by Cat Rock, a rocky outcropping on the left, and continue following the square metal blazes.

0.8 At trail junction HR 2, turn LEFT, continuing to follow the square metal blazes. After 50 yards, cross a small wooden bridge over a stream which runs into Storrow Pond on your right.

The stream you just crossed is Powissett Brook. If you were to follow this brook as it flows out the other end of Storrow Pond toward the border of the reservation, you would come upon the Powissett rockshelter, an overhanging rock ledge where in 1970 the remains of an Indian camp were discovered. Because the site was hidden from the trails that pass nearby, it was undisturbed and proved to be of great archaeological value. Excavations at the site indicate that the camp was probably used from 1580 to 1650 by Indians traveling to or from the coast. The rockshelter provided the Indians with a dry place to camp and to cook as they rested during their travels. Bones, shells and pottery shards found around here indicate that the Indians carried their food to this site in ceramic bowls, where they cooked and ate it. Their diet was quite varied — remains of deer, raccoon, porcupine, birds, turtles, fish, clams and mussels have been found at the site.

0.9 Turn RIGHT on a gravel road, continuing to follow the square metal blazes.

1.0 At a fork, bear LEFT, following the arrow toward Ohio Meadow.

If you are ready for a break, before making this turn, bear right on the short spur trail to Storrow Pond. The small dam at this end of the pond provides a sunny spot to rest and cool your toes in the cascade that runs underneath.

1.1 Bear LEFT at trail junction HR 3, following the square metal blazes.

The name Ohio Meadow is a curious artifact of the local eighteenth-century vernacular. After the American Revolution, a number of Massachusetts residents headed west to settle in the then-uncharted Ohio Territory. For the people who remained, the term "going to th' Ohio" came to mean heading off into the wilderness. The area of Hale Reservation that is now Ohio Meadow was originally cleared by the Powissett Indians and used for hunting, fishing and farming. As the nearby Dedham settlement expanded, the Indians were displaced and the meadow became a common pasture for new farms. These farms developed into the village of Dover and activity began to be centered around the meetinghouse in the middle of town, miles away from the pasture. The formerly convenient grazing land in the meadow was now only reachable by a rough trail through the woods. Complaining about the situation, local farmers would say, "I'd might as well go to th' Ohio as to bring m' cows way up to th' common pasture." The name stuck, and the Ohio Trail and Meadow are now recognized on the USGS map of the area. Although the meadow has since reverted to woods, you can still see the stone walls that once divided it into fields.

1.6 Continue STRAIGHT at trail junction HR 4, continuing to follow the square metal blazes. One hundred yards after you cross under the power lines, you will come to a clearing where the trail marked by square metal blazes continues straight and an unmarked trail bears off to the right. Bear RIGHT on this unmarked trail. You will no longer be following the square metal blazes. The trail will soon cross back under the power lines and continue through the woods. Follow this trail, bearing RIGHT at a fork just after crossing a stream on a plywood bridge.

2.0 At trail junction HR 5, turn RIGHT on a trail marked by metal triangles (Strawberry Hill Trail). Continue following the metal triangles through trail junctions HR 6 and 7.

At one time, the trail you are now on was a path that led from an Indian settlement along the Charles River in Dedham to Strawberry Hill, where you are now headed. The Powissett Indians would travel along this path to gather the wild strawberries that grew here. Fires set by the Indians kept the hill clear of trees and allowed the strawberries to flourish.

3.1 You reach an intersection where the trail marked by metal triangles turns left, marked by a post with a metal triangle and a left arrow, and 30 yards ahead on the left the trail is marked by a red circle and numbered 21. This is the edge of the Noanet Woodlands Reservation. Turn RIGHT up the hill, following the trail marked by red circles. Continue following the red circles and numbers in ascending order through number 33 (you will not see number 25).

From here the trail loops through Noanet Woodlands and returns to this same point. If you prefer a shorter ride, turn left here and continue to follow the metal triangles. In 0.5 mile, pick up the directions at mile 7.8.

4.3 Shortly after number 33, at a T intersection marked by a blue circle and the number 4, turn RIGHT. After 30 yards, at another T intersection, turn LEFT on a trail marked by yellow circles. Continue following the yellow circles and the numbers 5 through 18.

6.7 At number 18, bear RIGHT on a trail marked by red circles. Continue following the red circles and the numbers in ascending order to number 21.

7.3 At number 21, bear RIGHT onto a trail marked by metal triangles. You

reenter Hale Reservation here. Continue following the trail marked by metal triangles.

7.8 At trail junction HR 9, the trail marked by metal triangles bears left and an unmarked trail bears right. Bear RIGHT onto this unmarked trial. You will no longer be following the metal triangles.

8.1 The trail ends at a paved road. Turn LEFT on this road (Powissett Street).

8.5 Take your second LEFT on a paved road marked by a sign for Hale Reservation Family Membership Entrance.

8.7   At the end of the road, turn RIGHT, cross the parking lot and ride onto a narrow dirt trail that leads up a short hill into the woods. At the top of this short hill bear RIGHT, and after 30 yards bear LEFT. Continue on this narrow dirt trail through the woods.

9.2   As you reach a lodge, turn RIGHT onto a gravel road.

9.4   The gravel road runs into a parking lot (Cat Rock Parking Lot). Ride through the parking lot and turn RIGHT on the paved road (Carby Street).

9.7   You are back at the Hale Reservation office, where the ride began.

Additional Information
Hale Reservation, 80 Carby Street, Westwood, MA (508-326-1770). Open 9:00 a.m. to dusk.
Noanet Woodlands Ranger Station, Dedham Street, Dover, MA.
The Trustees of Reservations, 572 Essex Street, Beverly, MA 01915 (508-921-1944).

Bicycle Service
Bike Nashbar, 26 Wexford Street, Needham (617-444-6118). Sales, service.
Dedham Bike and Leather, 403 Washington Street, Dedham (617-326-1531). Sales, service, rentals.
Needham Cyclery, 240 Chestnut Street, Needham (617-444-9506). Sales, service.
Norwood Bicycle Depot, 85 Broadway, Norwood (617-762-2112). Sales, service.

Martha's Vineyard

Distance: 6.0 miles
Terrain: Flat forest trail and dirt path
Difficulty: Easy
Map: Manuel F. Correllus State Forest (available at headquarters); The Martha's Vineyard Map (published by The Butterworth Company; available in stores throughout the island)

Martha's Vineyard, the largest island on the southeastern coast of Massachusetts, is a bike rider's Utopia. Twenty miles long and nine miles wide, the island is small enough to be entirely accessible by bike but large enough to provide any number of interesting rides. The island was shaped by the receding glaciers of the last ice age, which left it with a variable terrain that makes it a pleasure to explore by bike. The coastline is defined by long sandy beaches interspersed with tidal estuaries and saltwater ponds that extend far inland. The interior of the island is forested woodland and marsh, perfectly flat in some places and hilly in others. With a mountain bike, you have easy access to the miles of dirt roads, trails and paved bike paths that extend to every corner of the island.

Even before the advent of the mountain bike, Martha's Vineyard was a popular place to visit. It has been theorized that the first summer tourists on the island were Norsemen, who visited in the first millennium. There are descriptions in Norse writings of a place called Vineland that suggest it could be none other than Martha's Vineyard. The earliest permanent residents were the Wampanoag, who called the island Noepe, meaning "in the midst of the sea." The first European who left written observations of the island was Bartholomew Gosnold, an Englishman who sailed from Europe in 1602 for the New World and landed at Cape Cod. From there, he sailed south, stopping at an island where he found "such an incredible store of [grape]vines, as well in the woodie part of the Island where they run upon every tree, as on the outward parts, that we could not goe for treading upon them." He named the island Martha's Vineyard. The abundant grapevines clearly inspired the Vineyard part of the name, but there are conflicting accounts as to whether the name Martha referred to Gosnold's mother, daughter or mother-in-law. After Gosnold's visit, almost 40 years passed before a

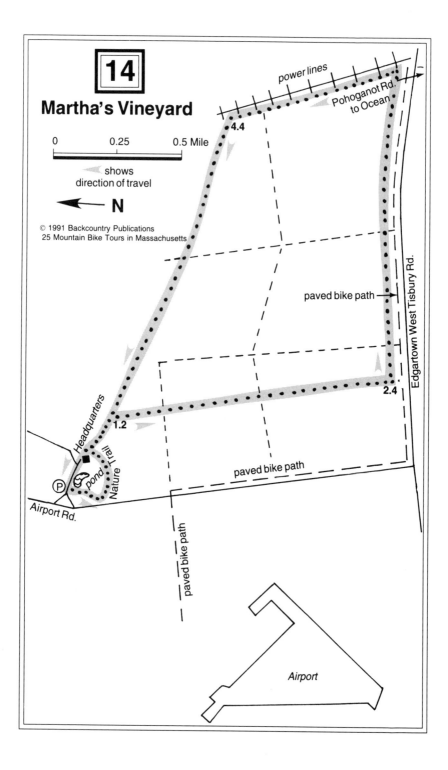

white settlement was established on the island. In 1641, Thomas Mayhew of Watertown, Massachusetts, purchased the Vineyard, Nantucket and the nearby Elizabeth Islands from two English noblemen for 40 pounds. Later that year, Mayhew's son established a settlement at what is now Edgartown. The settlement flourished and gradually other towns grew up around the island.

These early settlers made a prosperous living from fishing and farming, but it wasn't until the development of the whaling industry that Martha's Vineyard earned its place on the map. The Indians on the island had been whaling since before the white settlers came, and whales were so plentiful in Vineyard Sound that they could be caught from small boats just offshore. As this industry developed on the Vineyard the waters around the island became overfished, and the whalers had to build larger ships and go farther out for their catch. The first large whaling ship sailed from the Vineyard in 1765, and by the 1850's whalers were setting out for voyages lasting as long as five years. Edgartown was home to 50 whaling ships, and was one of the most important ports on the coast. The whaling industry thrived until the discovery of petroleum in 1859, which replaced whale oil as a fuel and thereby brought about the industry's gradual demise. The ship captains' houses that line the streets of Edgartown are reminders of the wealth and importance of the island during the whaling days.

With the decline of the whaling industry, the focus of the island's economy shifted to tourism. The Vineyard's popularity as a summer retreat began to grow in 1835, when a Methodist tent meeting was held at Oak Bluffs. These meetings were held every summer thereafter, and gradually the tents were replaced by the cottages from which the town developed. Today, tourism is the primary industry on the island, with the winter population of 12,000 increasing to 80,000 during the summer.

Because of the summer crowds, the best time to visit the Vineyard is in the off-season, spring or fall. The weather is still pleasant and the residents much more so once the tourist hordes have left. You can take a ferry to the island year round from Woods Hole, or from Falmouth, Hyannis or New Bedford during the spring, summer and fall. The Woods Hole ferry does carry cars, but it is easier to get around the island by bicycle. The three principal towns on the island—Vineyard Haven, Oak Bluffs and Edgartown—are within seven flat, smooth miles of one another and the ride along the coastline between them should not be missed. If you don't want to bring your own bike, you can easily rent one. Paved bike paths connect many points on the island, and if you don't feel like biking, there is a shuttle bus that runs between Vineyard Haven, Oak Bluffs and Edgartown from May to October.

From any of these three towns you have easy access to Manuel F. Correllus State Forest—4,000 acres of woodlands in the center of the island. The forest is crossed with trails, and a 14-mile paved bike path

Martha's Vineyard

runs along its perimeter. The terrain in the state forest is almost entirely flat, making for easy riding, although occasional sandy areas can be slow. The ride described here loops through one corner of the state forest and passes through a surprising variation of terrain, from open stands of tall white pine through blueberry and huckleberry thickets and onto sandy paths running between rows of stunted, gnarled pitch pines.

Other than the state forest, off-road riding on the island is limited since many trails run through private property. But there are numerous dirt roads on the island that are best explored by mountain bike. If you want to escape the summer crowds, take the one-minute ferry ride from Edgartown to Chappaquiddick Island and ride the dirt roads out to Wasque Point, a remote preserve of beach and sand dunes.

To Get There: The Manuel F. Correllus State Forest is in the middle of Martha's Vineyard, approximately five miles from Vineyard Haven, Oak Bluffs and Edgartown. To get there, get onto Airport Road, which runs through the center of the island. Follow Airport Road, then turn at the sign marked State Forest Headquarters onto an access road which runs to the headquarters.

The Ride

0.0 The ride starts on the Nature Trail near the state forest headquarters. Begin at the trailhead which is on the access road running between Airport Road and the headquarters. The trailhead is approximately 75 yards from Airport Road, next to a pond, and is marked by a sign marked Nature Trail. Start down this trail, which at this point is a wide, grassy path, and follow it as it leads into the woods.

0.3 Turn RIGHT at a grove of evergreens marked by a sign identifying them as red and white pines.

0.4 Turn LEFT at an airport lighting tower, following the signs for the Nature Trail.

0.6 Follow the trail as it turns LEFT, marked by a sign, and winds through an open stand of pruned white pine.

All the white pine that you see in the forest are relative newcomers to the island. The only native pine on Martha's Vineyard is the pitch pine, which is still one of the most common trees on the island. In many areas of the state forest, red pine was planted because it was thought that it would thrive in the sandy soil. However, almost all of these trees have been killed by a fungal disease, and the forest is being replanted with white pine and Norway spruce.

0.7 Continue STRAIGHT across an intersection with a wider trail, following the sign that points the way into a denser grove of spruce.

0.8 The trail emerges from the woods at the state forest headquarters. The marked Nature Trail ends here. Turn RIGHT, toward the headquarters, and after 50 yards, turn RIGHT again onto a dirt track opposite a blue shed. Follow the dirt track as it leads away from the headquarters, past trails intersecting from the left and right.

1.2 The track reaches an open field. Bear RIGHT at the fork at the corner of the field. Follow the track as it runs along the right edge of the field and continues into low trees, narrowing into a trail running more or less straight for 1.2 miles.

The bright sea-blue flowers with square petals you might see during the summer and fall as you ride through this field are chicory, also known as blue sailors, a plant that was brought from Europe and raised as a less-expensive substitute for coffee. The name of this plant comes from a legend about a woman who fell in love with a sailor who went off to sea, never to return. She wandered the roads, faithfully waiting for him to come back until the gods, taking pity, turned her into this plant, whose flowers still bloom along the roads she wandered.

2.4 Just before reaching a paved road, turn LEFT onto a narrow trail. The

Wasque Point, Chappaquiddick Island, Martha's Vineyard

trail is marked by a red triangular blaze on a tree 20 feet down the trail on the left. Follow this trail for 1.3 miles. It is well marked by red triangular blazes, and runs parallel to the road and a paved bike path on the right.

3.7   The blazed trail ends as it enters a cleared area with power lines overhead and a metal gate on the right marked with a number 9. Turn LEFT and follow the dirt track that runs underneath the power lines.

Near this corner of the state forest is a dirt road (Pohoganot Road) that runs south toward the ocean. There is also a dirt path nearby that heads east toward Edgartown. Take either of these two routes if you'd like to explore the island further.

4.4   Between the tenth and eleventh utility poles, turn LEFT onto a narrow trail that leads off diagonally into a thicket of bushes. Follow this trail for 1.3 miles to its end.

5.7   At the corner of an open field, the narrow trail ends as it joins the dirt track you started out on. Turn RIGHT on this track, and follow it back the way you came.

6.0   You are back at the state forest headquarters, where the ride began.

Additional Information

Manuel F. Correllus State Forest Headquarters (508-693-2540).

Martha's Vineyard Chamber of Commerce, Beach Road, Vineyard Haven, MA (508-693-0085).

The Steamship Authority, Woods Hole, MA (508-540-2022). Round trip Woods Hole–Vineyard Haven or Oak Bluffs, $8.00 per person, $5.50 per bicycle, $60 per automobile; parking $6.00 per day.

Hy-Line, Hyannis, MA (508-775-7185). Round trip Hyannis–Oak Bluffs, May to October, $20.00 per person, $8.00 per bicycle; parking $8.00 per day.

Island Queen, Falmouth, MA (508-548-4800). Round trip Falmouth–Oak Bluffs, May to October, $8.00 per person, $5.00 per bicycle; parking $6.00 per day.

New Bedford Ferry, New Bedford, MA (508-693-2088). Round trip New Bedford–Vineyard Haven, May to October, $16.00 per person, $4.00 per bicycle; parking $6.00 per day.

Bicycle Service

Cycle Works, 105 State Road, Vineyard Haven (508-693-6966). Sales, service.

Martha's Bike Rental, 4 Lagoon Pond Road, Vineyard Haven (508-693-6593). Sales, service, rentals.

Martha's Vineyard Scooter and Bike Rental, Union Street, Vineyard Haven (508-693-0782). Sales, service, rentals.

DeBettencourt's Bike Shop, Circuit Avenue, Oak Bluffs (508-693-0011). Rentals.

Sun 'n' Fun, Inc., Lake Avenue, Oak Bluffs (508-693-5457). Sales, service, rentals.

Vineyard Bike and Moped, Oak Bluffs Avenue, Oak Bluffs (508-693-4498). Rentals.

R.W. Cutter, Main Street, Edgartown (508-627-4052). Sales, service, rentals.

Nickerson State Park

Distance: 7.4 miles
Terrain: Rolling dirt path and forest trail, some connecting pavement
Difficulty: Easy to moderate
Map: Nickerson State Park (available at park headquarters)

Nickerson State Park is one of the last large tracts of forest left on Cape Cod and one of only a few spots on the Cape with enough open space to put together a substantial off-road ride. Although it is difficult to imagine today, the interior of Cape Cod used to be entirely covered by forest. When the first settlers arrived in the early seventeenth century, they quickly cleared the land, and by colonial times, demand for firewood and lumber had caused the demise of much of the Cape's woodlands. Over the following years, the increase of population in the growing towns on the narrow peninsula prevented the forests from growing back. More recently, tourism caused much of the remaining open land to be subdivided and developed, often eliminating what little forest was left. Although great efforts have been made to preserve public space on the Cape, most of what was spared from development was coastline and beach—great for swimming and tanning but not so great for mountain biking. Fortunately, Massachusetts was given 1,700 acres of forest land by the Nickerson family of Brewster in the 1930's, which it turned into Nickerson State Park. Today, Nickerson's rolling hills, its pine, oak and hemlock forests and freshwater ponds preserve a distinctive part of the Cape Cod landscape that has otherwise practically disappeared.

It is fitting that a Brewster family should make such a generous donation to the state, as the town was long home to many of Cape Cod's wealthiest residents. Settled in 1656, Brewster was originally part of the town of Harwich. As Harwich grew, its North Parish became populated by many of the town's more affluent residents, while poorer families were situated in the South Parish. In the early nineteenth century, North Parish petitioned the state legislature for permission to split off as a separate town. Although the ostensible reason for this split was to reduce the traveling distance to town meeting, in reality it was due to the economic disparity between the two parishes. A letter of protest written by South Parish residents to the legislature pointed out that 13 of the 15 Harwich paupers lived in South Parish, while 14 of the 15 "pleasure carriages" were owned by North Parish families. Thus, the wealthier North Parish wanted to become a separate town in order to avoid paying the tax required to support the poorer South Parish. Despite the objections from the residents of South Parish, North Parish split off from Harwich in 1803 and incorporated as the town of Brewster. Brewster's prosperity continued through the 1800's, supported by profitable saltworks and fishing industries, extensive cranberry bogs, and numerous wealthy sea captains and merchants who lived there.

Of all the well-to-do Brewster families, the wealthiest were the Nickersons, "Brewster's First Family," who summered there in the early part of this century. Samuel Nickerson, the patriarch, was a native of Cape Cod who made his fortune in Chicago and then returned to the Cape to build an estate. His son, Roland, expanded the family's extensive land holdings and soon become the largest private owner of forest land on Cape Cod. Roland and his wife Adele lived in Fieldstone Hall, an extravagant mansion built by Samuel in 1890 overlooking Cape Cod Bay. Besides vast gardens, its own electric generating plant and a windmill used for pumping water, it included cattle, horse and sheep farms as well as guest houses, a private beach with bathhouse and a Deer Park, a fenced-in game preserve where the family and friends hunted for deer, elk, bear, raccoon and fox. The Nickersons lived in Fieldstone Hall until May 24, 1906, when the mansion burned to the ground; two weeks later Roland Nickerson died. After recovering from these tragedies, Adele built an even larger mansion on the same site in 1908, this time of stone to ensure that it would be fireproof. It still stands, and is now the Ocean's Edge Conference Center, which can be seen about a mile west of the park entrance on MA 6A.

Nickerson State Park was created on the site of the Nickersons' Deer Park, which Adele donated to the state in 1934 in memory of her son, Roland C. Nickerson, Jr., who died of influenza during World War I. Today, the park is one of the most popular camping areas on the Cape, with more than 420 campsites situated around five ponds, and a network of paved and dirt roads, bike paths and hiking trails. Presently, mountain biking is allowed everywhere in the park except on designated hiking trails.

This ride circles the park along dirt roads, many of which have degraded into rough paths. The ride runs almost entirely through forest and passes a number of swimming ponds which are also stocked with trout and bass for fishing. Although some sections of the park are hilly, the riding is generally easy, the greatest difficulty coming from occasional patches of sand on the trails. If you find yourself getting stuck in one of these sand traps, shift your weight as far back as possible on the bike in order to increase the rear wheel's traction and to keep the front wheel from skidding.

To Get There: From MA 6, take exit 11 for MA 137, Brewster, Chatham. Follow MA 137 North for 3.7 miles, then turn right on MA 124

North. Follow MA 124 North for 0.4 mile, then turn right on MA 6A East. Follow MA 6A East for 2.9 miles, then turn right at the sign for Nickerson State Park. Ask at the contact station by the entrance for the best place to park, as restrictions vary seasonally.

The Ride

0.0   The ride begins from the contact station at the entrance. Start on the paved road (Deer Park Road) that runs from the contact station into the park.

0.3   Turn LEFT onto a paved road marked by signs for Area 5, Picnic Area, Public Beach, Boat Ramp.

1.4   One hundred yards before the paved road ends at a boat launch area, turn LEFT onto a dirt path.

1.8   Turn RIGHT on a sandy path, which runs downhill toward a pond visible through the trees.

1.9   As you reach the pond (Higgins Pond), bear RIGHT and go through a gate. Continue on this path as it follows along the pond's edge past trails intersecting from the right.

> The ponds in Nickerson State Park, like many on Cape Cod, are "kettle ponds" formed some 15,000 years ago when the last glacier to cover the Northeast retreated in the face of rapid global warming. As it receded, huge chunks of ice broke off and were covered with dirt and debris carried by meltwater streams. Eventually these cakes of ice melted and the debris covering them collapsed, leaving vast depressions known as kettle holes. Where these dipped below groundwater level, they became freshwater ponds. Because these ponds are not fed by springs or streams, their water level fluctuates greatly from season to season as rainfall and snowmelt raise or lower the groundwater level.
>
> The park's forests are of a more recent vintage and were created less "naturally" than the ponds, in that many of the trees grew from 88,000 white pine, spruce and hemlock seedlings planted there in the 1930's by the Civilian Conservation Corps.

2.4   Just as you reach the end of a smaller pond (Eel Pond) on the left, bear RIGHT at a sandy fork.

2.6   At the end of the dirt path, go through a gate and bear RIGHT onto a paved road, then turn immediately LEFT onto a paved bike path.

3.0   Just after the bike path crosses a paved road, bear LEFT at a fork onto a sandy path.

3.8   Bear RIGHT as a wider dirt road comes in from the left.

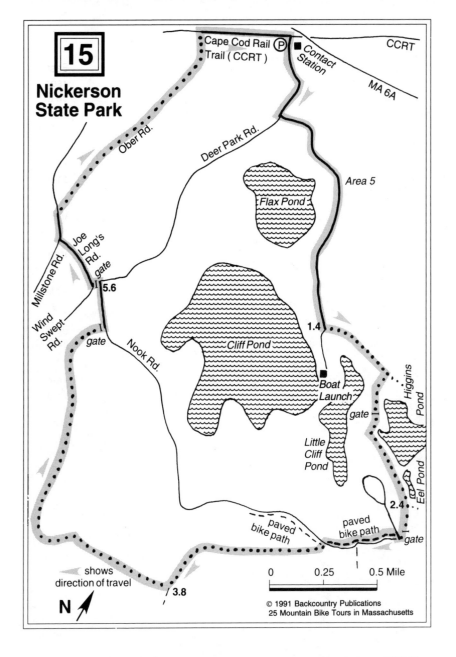

15

Nickerson State Park

Cape Cod Rail Trail (CCRT)

ⓟ

■ Contact Station

CCRT

MA 6A

Ober Rd.

Deer Park Rd.

Area 5

Flax Pond

Joe Long's Rd.

Millstone Rd.

gate

5.6

Wind Swept Rd.

gate

Nook Rd.

Cliff Pond

1.4

■ Boat Launch

gate

Little Cliff Pond

Higgins Pond

Eel Pond

2.4

paved bike path

paved bike path

gate

shows direction of travel

N

3.8

0   0.25   0.5 Mile

© 1991 Backcountry Publications
25 Mountain Bike Tours in Massachusetts

3.9 At a fork where a wide gravel road bears off to the left, bear RIGHT to stay on the sandy path.

5.5 At the end of the dirt path, go through a gate and turn LEFT onto a paved road (Nook Road).

5.6 At a sign on the left marked Area 6, Area 6 ext., Area 7, Overflow Area, turn LEFT, go through a gate and turn RIGHT onto a paved road (Joe Long's Road).

5.9 At the end of the road, turn RIGHT onto Millstone Road. After 100 yards, turn RIGHT onto a dirt path (Ober Road) that runs into the woods.

6.7 As the path you are on turns to sand, you may want to move onto a firmer trail running just to the right of the main path.

6.8 Cross under a set of power lines and continue STRAIGHT on the dirt path.

7.0 As you reach a paved bike path marked by a sign with a bicycle and the number 1 (Cape Cod Rail Trail), turn RIGHT.

This paved bike path is part of the Cape Cod Rail Trail, a 19.6-mile bikeway built along an abandoned railroad grade. It follows the route of the old Cape Cod Central Railroad, built in the early 1880's to service the then new tourist trade to Cape Cod. During the first half of this century, when the Cape was becoming a popular place to visit and trains were the preferred mode of travel, this rail line was used heavily. But as automobiles grew in popularity and car travel to the Cape was facilitated by the construction of bridges over the Cape Cod Canal, ridership on the railroad dropped, and by 1965 train service along the line stopped. In 1978, the Massachusetts Department of Environmental Management purchased the railroad right-of-way and converted it into a paved bike path. From the point where it passes by Nickerson State Park, the Cape Cod Rail Trail stretches 11.6 miles west to MA 134 in Harwich, and 7.9 miles east to the Salt Pond visitor center at the Cape Cod National Seashore in Eastham.

7.3 At a sign for Nickerson State Park, turn RIGHT. After 30 yards, turn LEFT and cross a parking lot.

7.4 You are back at the Nickerson State Park contact station, where the tour began.

Additional Information
Nickerson State Park, Route 6A, Brewster, MA (508-896-3491).

Bicycle Service
Summit Ski and Bike Shop, Route 6A, Orleans (508-255-7547). Sales, service.
Orleans Cycle, 52 Main Street, Orleans (508-255-9115). Sales, service, rentals.

Rocky Woods

Distance: Ride A — 2.7 mile
Ride B — 4.9 miles
Terrain: Ride A — Smooth, wide cinder and dirt paths, with frequent hills
Ride B — Mostly smooth, wide cinder and dirt paths, with some narrow
dirt trail; frequent hills with one steep climb and descent
Difficulty: Ride A — Easy to moderate
Ride B — Moderate to difficult
Map: Rocky Woods trail map (available at visitor center); USGS 7.5' × 15'
Medfield

Rocky Woods, a 490-acre forest reservation in Medfield owned by the
Trustees of Reservations, is an ideal spot for an afternoon of leisurely
mountain biking. The well-manicured grounds of the reservation encompass rolling hills, ponds and streams and are crisscrossed by 12 miles of
wide cinder paths. The smooth paths and gentle hills of Rocky Woods
make it easily accessible by bike, and the lush woods of the reservation
provide an appealing landscape through which to ride.

Rocky Woods' well-kept nature is characteristic of properties owned
by the Trustees of Reservations, an organization dedicated to protecting
the natural landscape by acquisition and maintenance of open land. The
largest private owner of conservation land in Massachusetts, with 70
properties totaling almost 18,000 acres, they acquired Rocky Woods
through land donations made to them over the last 50 years by a number
of Medfield residents. Besides woodlands like Rocky Woods, their holdings include beach areas, wildlife refuges and historic houses. Their
properties are very well managed and are open for hiking, nature study,
canoeing and other activities, usually for a small fee. Mountain biking is
allowed at some of the Trustees of Reservations properties, decided on a
case-by-case basis. By joining the organization, you receive a list indicating which properties allow mountain biking. Becoming a member also
gives you free admission to all properties.

Like many Trustees of Reservations areas, Rocky Woods is a popular place for families to come with children for a walk through the woods.
This fact, in addition to its wide, smooth trails, makes this area best suited
for slow-paced riding. It is a perfect place for a beginning mountain-
biker, as the wide trails are forgiving, but the frequent hills provide an
aerobic challenge. There is an informative self-guided nature trail at the

Echo Lake at Rocky Woods Reservation

reservation; guidebooks to it may be purchased at the visitor center on weekends. If you would like to explore this nature trail, please do so on foot, not on bicycle.

To Get There: From MA 128 (I-95) take exit 16B for 109 West, Westwood. Follow MA 109 West for 1.6 miles, then turn right onto Hartford Street. Follow Hartford Street for 3.2 miles, then turn right at the sign for Rocky Woods Reservation.

The Ride

Two overlapping rides are given for Rocky Woods. Ride A is a shorter one of three miles and stays on wide paths. More athletic riders may want to choose the five-mile ride B, which adds two hilly loops to ride A, one of which includes a short but strenuous climb and a steep, rocky descent. Both rides start and finish at the same place. The mileages given in the directions are only accurate for ride B.

0.0 **Rides A and B** The rides begin at the visitor center. Follow the path (Chickering Pond Trail) that starts in front of the visitor center and runs alongside the pond.

0.1 **Ride A** Continue STRAIGHT to trail junction 2, and skip to the directions at mile 0.6.

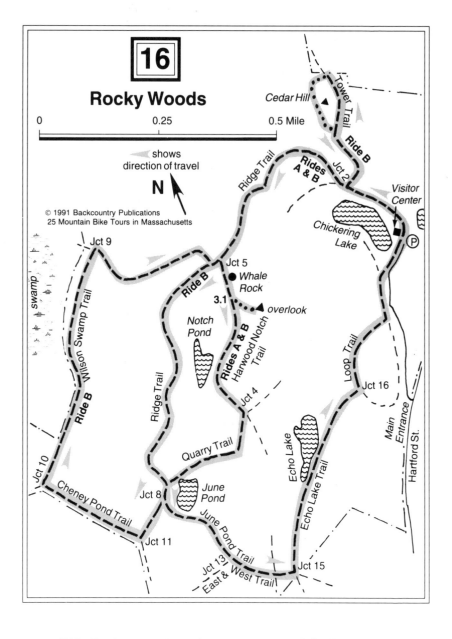

Ride B Just past the end of the pond, turn RIGHT on a path (Tower Trail) that climbs steeply up Cedar Hill.

0.4 At the top of the hill, bear LEFT at a fork. After 200 yards you reach a clearing at the top of Cedar Hill.

There was once an observation tower at the top of Cedar Hill, and you can still see the four foundation blocks set there. Even without the tower, there are still fine views of southern Massachusetts visible through the trees.

From the clearing at the top of the hill, turn LEFT onto a rocky dirt trail that descends steeply through the trees.

0.5 Turn RIGHT as you join up again with the path you ascended on. Continue back down the hill the way you came up. At the bottom of the hill, turn RIGHT.

0.6 At trail junction 2, bear RIGHT onto the Ridge Trail.

1.1 **Ride A** At trail junction 5, turn LEFT onto the Harwood Notch Trail. In 0.1 mile, pass Whale Rock on your left and skip to the directions at mile 3.0.

Ride B At trail junction 5, bear RIGHT to stay on the Ridge Trail. After 75 yards, at trail junction 6, bear LEFT to stay on the Ridge Trail.

1.7 At trail junction 8, bear RIGHT to stay on the Ridge Trail.

1.8 At trail junction 11, turn RIGHT onto the Cheney Pond Trail. Keep your eyes open for this turn as it is easy to miss.

2.1 At trail junction 10, bear RIGHT onto the Wilson Swamp Trail.

2.6 At trail junction 9, turn RIGHT to stay on the Wilson Swamp Trail.

2.9 At trail junction 6, turn LEFT onto the Ridge Trail. After 75 yards, at trail junction 5, turn RIGHT onto the Harwood Notch Trail.

3.0 You pass Whale Rock on your left.
If you stand in just the right place and squint a little bit, this huge outcrop of granite really does look like a giant humpback whale beached in the middle of the woods. The top of Whale Rock is an ideal spot for a summer picnic, and it is also a good place to view the process of natural succession, the means by which rock masses like this one break down and become fertile soil. Notice that the granite is covered in many places by small growths, called lichens. As the granite is worn down by erosion, grains of rock and dead lichen collect in crevices and form small pockets of soil. The soil in these crevices builds up and provides a foothold for more substantial mosses to grow. The erosion continues, the mosses decay, and increasing amounts of soil accumulate until there is enough to sustain ferns, then grasses, then shrubs and eventually trees. As this process continues, Whale Rock will be worn down to no more than a dolphin, its mass converted to soil giving life to the trees that surround it.

3.1 Bear LEFT on a grassy path that forks off the main trail. This is a dead end which leads to an overlook.

Rocky Woods

From this overlook you have a good view of the plains on which the town of Medfield was settled. Medfield's place in history is secured by its role in King Philip's War, a conflict over land rights between the Wampanoag Indians and the white settlers in New England. Although the Wampanoag had coexisted peacefully with the early settlers in this area, in the 1660's conflicts began to arise as more and more Indians were forced off their land by expanding settlements. Tensions escalated until 1675 when King Philip, the name given by white settlers to Metacomet, the leader of the Wampanoag, organized a number of tribes into an armed revolt. War broke out and the Indians began attacking isolated towns around New England.

At that time, Medfield was the farthest outlying settlement of Plymouth Colony, perched right on the border of Indian territory. Aware of its vulnerability, the town armed itself and called in support from surrounding towns. Despite this vigilance, on the night of February 21, 1675, Indian troops crept into the town and hid among the buildings. At daybreak, Samuel Morse, a Medfield resident, went to his barn to feed the cattle and discovered an Indian hidden there in the hay. As he fled in surprise, the barn was set on fire. This was a signal for the attack to commence, and soon buildings all over town were burning. By the end of the fighting, half the town had burned to the ground and 15 settlers had been killed.

Many villages, fields and forests throughout New England were destroyed in similar ways during King Philip's War, which lasted until 1676, when the Indians, outnumbered, were overpowered. King Philip, holding out until the end, was killed at his home in Rhode Island. This war was the New England Indians' last futile attempt to keep the land that had been theirs. Subsequently, the colonists ruled the land, and those Indians who had not been killed or sold into slavery were restricted to reservations.

After visiting the overlook, return the way you came, down the grassy path. When you join the main trail, turn LEFT, heading down the hill.

3.5   At trail junction 4, turn RIGHT onto the Quarry Trail.

3.8   At trail junction 8, turn LEFT onto the June Pond Trail.

4.0   At trail junction 13, bear LEFT onto the East and West Trail.

4.1   At trail junction 14, continue STRAIGHT to stay on the East and West Trail. After 100 yards, at trail junction 15, bear LEFT onto the Echo Lake Trail.

4.6   At trail junction 16, bear LEFT onto the Loop Trail.

4.9   You are back at the visitor center, where the tour began.

Additional Information

Rocky Woods Reservation, Hartford Street, Medfield, MA (508-359-6333). Open Wednesday to Sunday, 10:00 a.m. to 6:00 p.m. Visitor center open only on weekends. Admission $1.00; children under six and members of the Trustees of Reservations, free.

The Trustees of Reservations, 572 Essex Street, Beverly, MA 01915 (508-921-1944).

Bicycle Service

Town and Country Bicycles, 67 North Street, Medfield (508-359-8377). Sales, service.

Wompatuck State Park

Distance: 8.2 miles
Terrain: Flat to rolling dirt path and forest trail, with some connecting pavement
Difficulty: Easy to moderate
Map: Wompatuck State Park (available at visitor center); USGS 7.5′ × 15′ Weymouth

Wompatuck State Park is the largest link in a chain of park land that extends through Hingham and Cohasset, two towns that pride themselves on their land conservation efforts. The park came to these towns in the late 1960's as a "peace dividend" from the U.S. government. Originally used by the Navy to store ammunition during World War II and the Korean War, the land comprising Wompatuck was given to the state when it was no longer needed by the armed services. Massachusetts turned this property into a state park which today encompasses over 2,800 acres of open space. Within it are hiking trails, bridle paths and paved bicycle paths, as well as ponds, a 400-acre camp site and a nature study area.

The park was named after Sachem Wompatuck, leader of the Massachuset tribe that controlled Massachusetts Bay from Swampscott to Duxbury. The Massachuset were a semi-nomadic tribe that moved from camp to camp according to the seasons. In spring they lived near fields where they planted corn, vegetables and other crops. During summer most moved to the coast where they fished and gathered shellfish, while some remained at the fields to tend the plantings. In fall the fish, corn and vegetables gathered during the summer were dried and preserved to sustain the tribe during winter, when they moved to warmer inland valleys.

When Sachem Wompatuck took over the leadership of the Massachuset in 1633, the tribe was in great decline. They had been struck by a devastating plague in 1616, which historians estimate wiped out 95 percent of their population. In 1635, a group of colonists led by Peter Hobart, a Puritan minister from the English town of Hingham, established a plantation on the coast south of Boston. These settlers found the Indians friendly and helpful, providing them with food, helping them to grow corn, and happily signing treaties with the strong, well-armed white men. With the Indians' support, the Puritans divided the land, built a

village, and incorporated it as Hingham, the twelfth town to be recognized by the Massachusetts Bay Colony.

More settlers followed, and by 1639 Hingham's population had reached 200. The town, inhabited mainly by farmers and artisans, continued to prosper and by the Revolution it had grown to almost 2,000 people. In the 1800's, Hingham thrived on the strength of its fishing and trading industries. It became a major port of entry for cargo destined for nearby Boston, and a succession of steamboats, and later railroad cars, brought goods to Boston's downtown markets. During the 1900's these industries declined, but the wealth they provided is still evident in the many fine old houses throughout the town, today a quiet residential suburb of Boston.

The land on which Wompatuck State Park is located remained mostly unused throughout much of Hingham's history. The early settlers used the forests of Wompatuck for woodlots and pasture, and in the 1700's a shingle mill was built on one of its streams, but it wasn't until 1941 that the land was substantially developed. In that year, as the U.S. was gearing up for World War II, the Navy took over 3,800 acres of open land in Hingham and Cohasset for use as a storage annex for the nearby Hingham Naval Ammunition Depot. Massive bunkers were built on the property and a series of roads and railroads were constructed to move equipment. The government held the land until 1967, when it sold most of it to the state, retaining 753 acres for an army reserve center.

This ride follows a wide bridle path in a loop that runs through half of the park. Besides the trails followed on this tour, there are few other unpaved paths in the park. However, if you're not dead set on riding on dirt, you can extend your ride by using the widespread system of paved bike paths that crisscrosses the park.

To Get There: From MA 3, take exit 14 for MA 228, Rockland, Nantasket. Follow MA 228 North for 4.1 miles, then turn right onto Free Street, following the sign for Wompatuck State Park. Follow Free Street for 0.8 mile, then turn right onto Union Street at the sign for Wompatuck State Park. Follow Union Street into the park for 0.4 mile, then turn right into the visitor center parking lot.

The Ride

0.0   The ride begins from the visitor center. Leave the visitor center parking lot and turn RIGHT on the paved road which runs into the park (Union Street).

0.2   Turn RIGHT on a paved road which leads back into the visitor center parking lot. After 30 yards turn LEFT on a dirt path marked by a sign Cross Country Skiing Only. After a few hundred yards, bear LEFT at a fork.

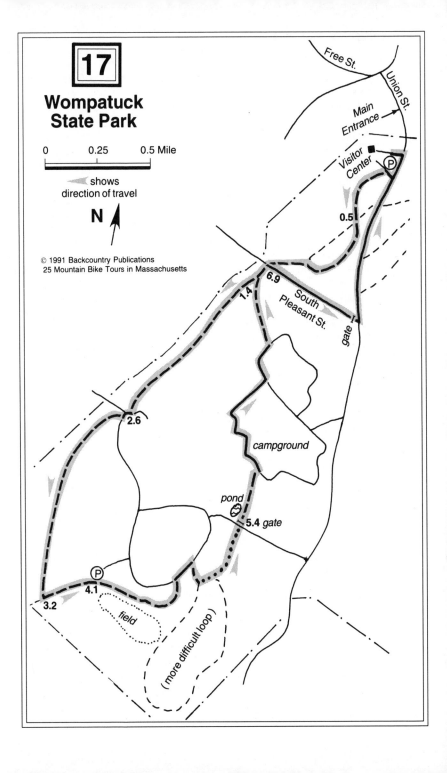

0.5 At a four-way intersection, continue STRAIGHT on a trail blazed by white circles.

Along this part of the ride you might notice the smooth, rounded rockfaces pushing up through the forest floor. These outcroppings are Dedham granodiorite, a rock very similar to the Quincy granite quarried in nearby towns. Because it is unique, durable and aesthetically pleasing, it has been called a mason's dream stone. What makes this particular granite so popular for stonework is its exact proportions of quartz, felspar, mica and hornblende. If you look closely you can see these individual crystals; their large size is an indication that the rock was formed deep underground and cooled slowly and under intense pressure. Geologists believe that this granite, which forms the underlying bedrock of much of the local area, is what remains of a vast mountain range pushed up from the earth hundreds of millions of years ago, then worn down to almost nothing by centuries of erosion.

0.6 Bear RIGHT onto a paved bicycle path which soon turns to dirt. After 100 yards, bear RIGHT at a fork. Continue on this path, following the white blazes through successive intersections.

0.9 At a fork, bear RIGHT.

1.4 Bear RIGHT at a fork and continue on the dirt path.

2.6 As the dirt path ends, bear RIGHT on a roughly paved road. In 0.1 mile, at an intersection with a paved path leading off to the left, turn RIGHT on a narrow trail marked by a white arrow pointing in the opposite direction from which you are heading.

3.2 At a T intersection by a fence that marks the park boundary, turn LEFT.

4.1 When the path you are on runs into a parking lot at the end of a paved road, turn RIGHT. Cross the parking lot and proceed across the field that is directly ahead, staying along the left edge of the field.

4.3 As you reach the back left corner of the field, turn LEFT onto a wide path that runs into the woods.

4.5 As you reach a paved road, turn RIGHT.

4.7 Turn RIGHT on a dirt road. After 30 yards, turn LEFT on a path running uphill. Near the top of the hill, as the main path continues straight ahead, turn LEFT onto a narrow trail that runs into the woods.

If you would prefer to extend your ride, instead of turning left here on the narrow trail that runs into the woods, continue straight on the main path. This path loops around and eventually reconnects with the tour route. The trail covered on this loop is rockier and more difficult than the other trails on this ride, and adds 1.5 miles to the total distance.

5.1 At a T intersection, turn RIGHT.

5.4 As you reach a paved road, turn LEFT. After 30 yards, turn RIGHT and go through a metal gate onto a dirt path that leads toward a pond. Continue on this path as it runs alongside the pond.

5.8 As you reach a paved road, turn LEFT.

6.0 At a fork, bear LEFT.

6.1 At a fork, bear LEFT. After a few hundred yards, bear LEFT on a dirt and broken pavement road.

6.3 At a paved road, turn LEFT.

6.4 As the road curves around to the RIGHT, bear LEFT on a dirt path running into the woods.

6.9 As you reach a paved path, turn RIGHT (South Pleasant Street).

7.5 Go through a gate and turn LEFT onto a paved road (Union Street). As you ride along this road, you pass a number of paved paths leading off to the right. A right turn on any one of these will take you into a network of bicycle paths that weave around the abandoned buildings and half-buried concrete bunkers of the former Naval Ammunition Depot. This area is interesting to explore, but be sure to leave enough time to find your way out of the somewhat confusing maze of paths. At one end of the park, these paved bike paths run into an area still used as an army reservation. Beyond that, they connect with the trail network of Whitney and Thayer Woods, a park owned by the Trustees of Reservations, which offers additional off-road riding possibilities.

8.2 You are back at the visitor center parking lot, where the tour began.

Additional Information
Wompatuck State Park, Union Street, Hingham, MA (617-749-7160).

Bicycle Service
Quinn's Bicycle Shop, 15 North Street, Hingham (617-749-0108). Sales, service.
The Bicycle Link, 230 Washington Street (Route 53), Weymouth (617-337-7125). Sales, service.
Cohasset Cycle Sports, 113 Ripley Road, Cohasset (617-383-0707). Sales, service.
Freewheelin' Cyclery, 38 North Street, Hingham (617-749-9760). Sales, service.

Harvard Forest

Distance: 15.1 miles
Terrain: Rolling dirt path and dirt road with some connecting pavement
Difficulty: Moderate
Map: USGS 7.5′ × 15′ Athol

About 70 miles from its main campus in Cambridge, Harvard University has a second outpost of higher education, this one covered with pine and oak instead of ivy. The Harvard Forest in Petersham consists of 3,000 acres of land owned by Harvard University and used for field research in forestry and forest biology. Whereas most forests normally are publicized in terms of their picnic groves and scenic views, Harvard's is proclaimed as being "located . . . in the New England upland physiographic region, . . . [its] varied topography contain[ing] a wide range of microclimates. These combine with soil differences to create a set of habitats that span almost the whole New England spectrum including northern, transition and central forest types, marshes, hardwood swamps and conifer bogs and a 25 hectare lake." But its academic leanings don't prevent the forest from being a good spot to mountain bike. The dirt roads that run through the forest connect with a network of old cart paths that cross Petersham. By linking these two trail systems, it is possible to put together a long and interesting mountain bike ride.

The forest was given to Harvard in 1907 by donors interested in forestry and forest biology. Since 1914, when the university established a graduate program in forestry, the Harvard Forest has been the central field site for demonstration, teaching and research. Closely studied for over eighty years, a remarkable amount of data has been collected on land use and changes in vegetation in the forest, and it is one of the oldest consistently managed and studied forests in the United States, making it a unique laboratory for natural scientists.

The facilities include labs, classrooms, dormitories and the Fisher Museum of Forestry, which houses a fascinating series of dioramas that portray the history of New England forests and explain the impact man and nature have had on them since the seventeenth century. There are also two self-guided nature trails, the Black Gum Trail and the Natural History Trail. Placards placed along these trails explain the natural history and forest biology of the area. Maps and guides are available at the Fisher Museum.

This ride starts on the dirt roads that run through the Harvard Forest, and then connects with a network of dirt roads and paths running through Petersham. Although these roads and paths are public, in many cases the land along which they run is private, so please stay on the trails to avoid trespassing.

To Get There: From MA 2, take the exit for MA 32, Athol, Petersham. Follow MA 32 South for 2.7 miles, then turn left at the sign for Harvard Forest. After 40 yards, turn right and park in the lot in front of the Fisher Museum of Forestry.

The Ride

0.0 The ride begins from the parking lot in front of the Fisher Museum of Forestry. From this lot, turn RIGHT on the dirt road that runs into Harvard Forest, passing between a white house on the left and the museum on the right. Continue on this road past trails intersecting from both left and right.

> The white house to the left is an old farmhouse, built when Harvard Forest was a working farm. Located on land granted in 1733 to the early settlers of Petersham in compensation for their services in the Indian wars, the land was purchased by Jonathan Sanderson in 1763, when Petersham was a frontier town and still about 90 percent forested. Sanderson began carving out a homestead, and in 1806 his son, John Sanderson, inherited the property. He cleared the land and built it into a productive and prosperous farm. Farming in the sandy, rocky New England soil was hard, slow work, but during the time that John Sanderson was running his farm numerous industrial communities were springing up in the area. These mill towns stimulated a great demand for farm products to fill their markets and feed their workers, guaranteeing a strong market and high prices for farmers. Taking advantage of this need, the Sanderson family became quite wealthy. The economic benefits of farming were felt throughout the area, and by 1830 approximately 80 per-

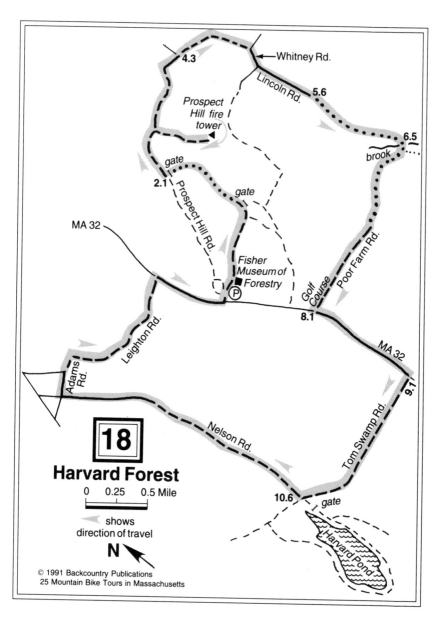

Prospect Hill fire tower

Whitney Rd.

Lincoln Rd.

4.3

5.6

6.5

brook

gate

2.1

gate

Prospect Hill Rd.

MA 32

Fisher Museum of Forestry

Golf Course

Poor Farm Rd.

Leighton Rd.

8.1

MA 32

9.1

Adams Rd.

Tom Swamp Rd.

Nelson Rd.

10.6

gate

Harvard Pond

18

Harvard Forest

0   0.25   0.5 Mile

shows direction of travel

N

© 1991 Backcountry Publications
25 Mountain Bike Tours in Massachusetts

cent of the land in the Petersham area had been cleared of trees and was being cultivated.

Farming in Petersham continued to be good business until 1830, when the opening of the Erie Canal changed the face of agriculture in New England. It now became convenient to ship farm products from the Midwest to the East. Farmers in the fertile land of the Midwest were able to grow crops in greater quantity and far more cheaply than farmers in the Northeast, and in the face of this competition New England farms ceased to be profitable. Many farmers were forced to give up their land and find new jobs. The Sandersons, anticipating the coming decline in the farm business, sold their property while it was still valuable and used the capital to found a bank. Their farmland, which had taken years of labor to clear, sat unnoticed for the next 60 years while it was slowly taken over by forests of fast-growing pine.

In the early 1900's, to the surprise of many landowners, a new economic use was discovered for this abandoned farmland. The growing industrial society of the time, not yet having discovered plastic, required wood to construct the boxes, barrels and buckets that were essential for daily life. Hundreds of factories in New England were turning out these products in quantity, and a large percentage of these factories were located within a few miles of Petersham. The wood supplying these factories came from the vast stands of white pine that had proliferated on the formerly cultivated land. Owners of this land found themselves in possession of a "voluntary" crop worth a great deal of money, and sale of this lumber brought a new prosperity to Petersham that has carried it down to the present.

0.9 At a fork marked by a metal gate 150 yards up the right branch, bear LEFT to stay on the dirt road as it curves around to the left. Continue on this road as it narrows to a dirt path.

As you ride through this part of the forest you pass groves of trees that have been thinned or clear-cut as part of Harvard's research effort. Study of the forest has reflected changing concerns in forest management. In the early 1900's, the focus was primarily on management to attain economic goals: maximizing timber production and maintaining the forest as a self-supporting lumber business. Since World War II, however, researchers have begun taking a broader perspective, viewing the forest as a source of clean water, a home for wildlife and a place for recreation.

In order to learn how the forest is affected by both man and nature, researchers use Harvard Forest as a living laboratory of forest biology. For example, a number of trees in one stand have been knocked over to simulate hurricane damage, and scientists have been recording the root mass dimensions, trunk angles and light, moisture and wind conditions around these trees. This information will lead to a better understanding of how storms can change the forest.

2.1 Pass through a metal gate and turn RIGHT onto a dirt road.

2.4 At a fork, bear RIGHT onto a dirt road (Prospect Hill Road). This is a spur trail to the top of Prospect Hill.

3.0   You reach the top of Prospect Hill.

At the top of Prospect Hill is an old fire tower, one of many that Massachusetts once maintained as part of a system for detecting and fighting forest fires. Observers were stationed in these towers from April to October and were equipped with two-way radios to keep in touch with local fire wardens. When a forest fire was detected, the observer notified the local fire warden and fire trucks were dispatched to the scene. Today, many of the towers are no longer used, as it is cheaper and more effective to patrol the forests from airplanes.

After taking in the view from Prospect Hill, return back the way you came down the access road.

3.6   At the end of the Prospect Hill access road, turn RIGHT.

4.1   At the end of the dirt road, turn RIGHT onto a paved road.

4.3   As the paved road curves sharply left, continue STRAIGHT on a dirt road marked by a sign for Prospect Hill. Follow this dirt road as it runs downhill.

4.9   As you reach a paved road, turn RIGHT (Whitney Road).

5.1   At a fork, bear LEFT on a road marked by a sign saying Dead End Road (Lincoln Road).

5.6   At the end of the paved road, continue STRAIGHT on a dirt path.

The dirt roads and paths you are riding on are part of an intricate series of connecting and feeder roads built in Petersham in the early 1800's, when most of the land was being farmed and these roads were necessary for taking farm equipment to the fields and getting crops out to market. Very few parts of town at the time were more than a quarter of a mile from some kind of road. Today, although some of these roads have been paved and others have grown over, many are still accessible by bike and can be found on the USGS map.

6.5   After crossing a stream on a bridge made of smooth, flat stones, continue STRAIGHT for 75 yards to a fork. At the fork, bear RIGHT. Continue on this dirt path as it widens into a dirt road (Poor Farm Road).

7.9   Watch out for golf balls as you pass through a golf course.

8.1   When the dirt road ends at a paved parking lot next to a white building (Petersham Curling Club), go through the parking lot, and at the end of the driveway turn LEFT onto a paved road (MA 32).

9.1   As you descend a hill, turn RIGHT onto a dirt road (Tom Swamp Road). This is your first possible right, but it can be difficult to find because a number of dirt driveways turn off to the right before it.

10.6 At a four-way dirt road intersection marked by a gate with a sign for Harvard Forest on the left, turn RIGHT (Nelson Road).

A left turn here through the gate will bring you into another tract of the Harvard Forest. If you would like to extend your ride and explore a little, turn left here and follow the trails that run around Harvard Pond.

12.1 Continue STRAIGHT as the dirt road turns to pavement.

12.9 At a four-way intersection, turn RIGHT (Adams Road).

13.1 As the paved road turns left, continue STRAIGHT on a dirt road (Leighton Road).

14.5 At the end of the dirt road, turn RIGHT onto a paved road (MA 32).

15.1 At the sign for Harvard Forest, turn LEFT. You are back at the Fisher Museum of Forestry, where the tour began.

Additional Information

Fisher Museum of Forestry, MA 32, Petersham, MA (508-724-3302). Open weekdays 9:00 a.m. to 5:00 p.m. year round, Saturdays 10:00 a.m. to 4:00 p.m. May to October, closed Sundays and holidays.

Bicycle Service

O'Neil's Bicycle Shop, 108 Main Street, Gardner (508-632-7200). Sales, service.

Otter River State Forest

Distance: 18.5 miles
Terrain: Rolling to hilly dirt path, dirt road and forest trail, with some connecting pavement
Difficulty: Moderate to difficult
Map: USGS 7.5′ × 15′ Winchendon; Otter River State Forest (available at state forest headquarters)

On the northern fringe of central Massachusetts, not far from the New Hampshire border, lies a vast area of abandoned forest. Back in the days when farming was a viable way to make a living in Eastern Massachusetts, this land was settled, plotted, cleared and cultivated; when farms were replaced by factories and people moved into cities, it fell out of use and was eventually reclaimed by forest. Today, the once productive fields and pastures are no longer visible, and the rutted dirt roads and crumbling stone walls that divide the forest into neat squares offer the only evidence of the land's prior use. Far enough away from civilization that many of the roads traversing it remain unpaved, this area offers some of the best long-distance off-road riding to be found. The old dirt roads that once took workers to the fields and crops to market now provide an abundance of routes for exploring the backwoods of Massachusetts by mountain bike.

This ride follows these old dirt roads as they wind through the towns of Winchendon and Royalston. It begins at the Otter River State Forest, a 1,200-acre tract of woodlands in Winchendon, crosses the forest, and then continues in a broad loop through the western part of Winchendon and South Royalston, weaving in and out of the Birch Hill Wildlife Management Area along the way. The farther this ride gets from the starting point, the rougher and more desolate the trails become. At first, most of the riding is along maintained dirt roads. As you move out of the state forest and into the Birch Hill area, they degrade into rutted paths and then rough trails, and you find yourself riding through stretches of forest that seem as if no one has visited in a long, long time.

The roads on this ride are just a few of the many that traverse the countryside around Winchendon and Royalston. This network extends well across the border into New Hampshire and it is possible to put together a much longer, or much shorter, ride than the one given here. Because of the remoteness of these roads, it is important to bring along the USGS map of the area (the Otter River State Forest trail map shows only some of the trails covered on this ride). Be aware, however, that the USGS map can be inaccurate at times. For example, most of the roads on this ride are designated by the same thin line indicating "unimproved road," but in actuality they vary from smooth, wide dirt roads to barely visible forest trails. Also be aware that the USGS maps are often incomplete or out of date, especially when it comes to showing smaller trails or recently constructed roads. Despite these limitations, the USGS map is still useful and is the best source of route information on this area.

Hunting is allowed in wildlife management areas, so use caution in Birch Hill during the hunting season. You can call the Otter River State Forest headquarters for information on the level of hunting activity in the forest at the time you are planning to visit.

To Get There: From MA 2, take the exit for US 202 North, Phillipston, Winchendon. Follow 202 North for 4.7 miles, then turn left at the sign for Otter River State Forest. After 50 yards, turn left into the state forest headquarters parking lot.

The Ride

0.0   The ride begins at the state forest headquarters parking lot. From this lot, turn LEFT onto the paved road that runs into the state forest. After 20 yards, go through a gate and continue STRAIGHT on this road.

0.4   As you reach the parking lot for the Beamon Pond Campground, continue STRAIGHT across the parking lot and onto the road that runs out the other side. Just after leaving the parking lot, at a fork marked by a Nature Trail sign pointing to the right, bear LEFT and in 30 yards, at another fork, bear LEFT following the sign for campsites 17-28.

0.6   At the end of the paved path, go through a brown and yellow metal gate and turn RIGHT onto a dirt road.

0.9   At a fork, bear LEFT.

1.0   Continue STRAIGHT as you pass by a cemetery on the right. After 0.1 mile, at an intersection turn RIGHT onto a rough paved road, and continue STRAIGHT past roads intersecting from the left and right.

The cemetery you pass here is that of New Boston, a section of one of Central Massachusetts' many "lost" villages. First settled around 1780, New Boston tried to establish itself as a town in 1794 by annexing sections of Winchendon, Royalston, Templeton and Phillipston. This attempt at secession failed, and New Boston remained a neighborhood of Winchendon.

New Boston was primarily a residential area, its only industries being a few small farms, a sawmill and a woodworking factory. It gained some notoriety in 1930 when three Gardner men purchased

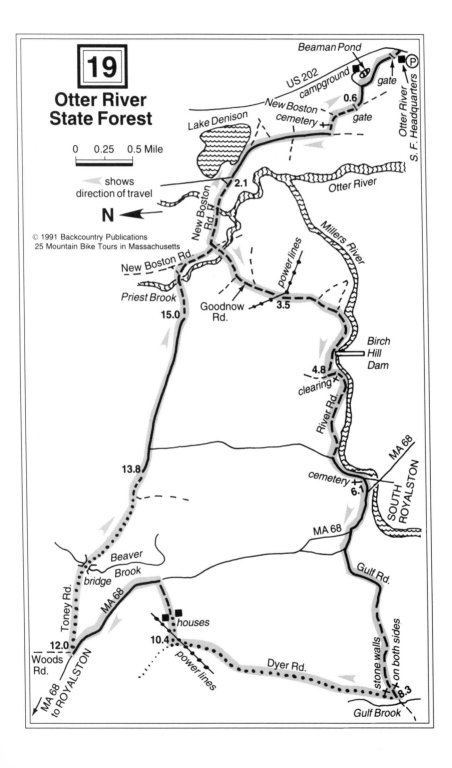

19
Otter River State Forest

Beaman Pond

US 202

campground

0.6

gate

gate

New Boston cemetery

S. F. Headquarters

Otter River

P

Lake Denison

0   0.25   0.5 Mile

shows
direction of travel

N

© 1991 Backcountry Publications
25 Mountain Bike Tours in Massachusetts

2.1

New Boston Rd.

Otter River

Millers River

New Boston Rd.

Priest Brook

15.0

Goodnow Rd.

power lines

3.5

Birch Hill Dam

4.8

clearing

River Rd.

13.8

MA 68

cemetery

6.1

SOUTH ROYALSTON

MA 68

Beaver Brook

bridge

Gulf Rd.

Toney Rd.

MA 68

houses

10.4

power lines

Dyer Rd.

stone walls on both sides

12.0

Woods Rd.

MA 68 to ROYALSTON

8.3

Gulf Brook

90 acres of open land near the center of the village and built the Happy Landings Airport. The airport included a cartwheel-type runway so that planes could land from any direction and hangers to house two biplanes and a monoplane.

In the late 1930's the United States government began construction on a flood control dam on the Millers River in Royalston, taking almost all of the land in New Boston to create a reservoir for the flood waters. Homes were deserted, the church was torn down, and roads closed. Today, all that remains of the abandoned village is its graveyard.

1.8 You reach Lake Denison on the right.

Lake Denison is a camping and recreation area associated with the Otter River State Forest. The lake was named after a man named Denison who, "lost in the woods, climbed a tree to command a wider range of prospect, and thus discovered the gleaming waters of the beautiful lake . . . which after him took the name of Denison Pond." In the late 1800's and early 1900's, the lake was a popular resort area, with cottages around the shore, a dancing pavilion and a steam launch that provided tours of the lake. With the implementation of the Birch Hill Flood Control Project in the 1940's, the land around the lake was appropriated by the federal government and the cottages were removed. Today it is a park, equipped with campsites, picnic areas and facilities for swimming and boating.

2.1 Bear LEFT off the paved road onto a wide dirt road marked New Boston Road, Royalston.

2.8 Turn LEFT onto a dirt road (Goodnow Road), and after 50 yards bear RIGHT at a fork. Continue STRAIGHT on this dirt road past roads intersecting from the left and right.

3.5 At a fork underneath a set of power lines, bear LEFT, and then continue STRAIGHT on this dirt road.

4.5 You pass by the Birch Hill Dam on the left.

In 1936, the town of Winchendon experienced a devastating flood when melting snow and torrential downpours caused the Millers River to overflow its banks, taking out bridges, dams and roads, paralyzing the town for weeks. Two years later, while the town was still rebuilding from this disaster, it was ravaged again by floods during the great hurricane of September 1938. In the wake of these disasters, the federal government constructed a flood control project in the Millers River watershed. It acquired 8,500 acres of land in Winchendon and Royalston, and in 1940 the Army Corps of Engineers began constructing the Birch Hill Dam, completing it in 1942. The dam, which rises 56 feet above the level of Millers River, holds back water during times of heavy rain to prevent it from overflowing its banks. The federal government owns 4,600 acres around the dam, which is leased to the state as flood control acreage and, as such, is "subject to inundation during flood operations." The balance of the land taken for the project is now owned outright by the state and operated as the Birch Hill Wildlife Management Area.

4.8 Just after descending a small hill to a clearing, bear LEFT to stay on the main road (River Road) as it curves to the left back toward the dam. Continue on this road as it curves back to the right and runs alongside a river (Millers River) to the left.

5.8 As you reach the end of the dirt road at a point where the river curves to the left, turn LEFT onto a paved road that continues to run alongside the river.

6.1 At a cemetery, turn RIGHT.

6.3 At the bottom of a hill, bear RIGHT as you join in with a road coming in from the left (MA 68).

6.6 Watch for a plaque on the right commemorating the Old Schoolhouse. Fifty yards after passing this plaque, as the road curves around to the right, bear LEFT at a fork (Gulf Road).

6.8 At a fork identified by a yellow diamond-shaped sign marked Plantation on the right, bear LEFT.

7.4 Continue STRAIGHT as the road turns to dirt.

8.3 At an intersection marked by stone walls along both sides, turn RIGHT onto a rutted dirt path (Dyer Road) that cuts sharply back to the right. Continue STRAIGHT on this path past trails intersecting from the left and right.
    Watch carefully for this turn, as it is easy to miss. Although this road is shown on the map as the first right turn, there are unmarked dirt roads leading off to the right before this one. If you pass over a narrow brook (Gulf Brook) which runs underneath the road, you have gone 150 yards too far.

10.4 Continue STRAIGHT as the trail crosses under a set of power lines. After a few hundred yards, at a fork, bear RIGHT and cross back under the power lines onto a path that runs uphill.

10.7 Continue STRAIGHT as the path reaches a group of houses and widens to a dirt road.

10.9 At the end of the dirt road, turn LEFT onto a paved road (MA 68).

12.0 Just after passing a sign for Windfall Farms on the left, and just before a road (Woods Road) forks off to the right, turn RIGHT onto a grassy trail

(Toney Road) that cuts back sharply to the right. The entrance to this trail is somewhat overgrown and may be not be obvious. Continue on this trail as it climbs through the woods.

12.3 Bear LEFT as a trail joins in from the right.

12.7 Continue STRAIGHT as you cross over a brook. A small plywood bridge is sometimes in place over this brook. If the bridge has washed out, you may have to cross the brook on two fallen logs about 100 feet downstream.

13.4 Bear LEFT as you join a dirt road coming in from the right. Continue STRAIGHT past roads intersecting from left and right.

13.8 Continue STRAIGHT as the road turns to pavement.

15.0 Continue STRAIGHT as the road turns back to dirt.

15.5 Bear RIGHT onto a wide dirt road (New Boston Road) coming in from the left.

From this point you will be backtracking to the Otter River State Forest along the same roads you came out on.

16.5 Bear RIGHT onto a paved road coming in from the left.

17.5 At an intersection, turn LEFT onto the dirt road that runs past the New Boston cemetery on your left.

17.9 Bear LEFT through the brown and yellow metal gate onto the paved path that leads into the Beamon Pond campground.

18.1 Continue STRAIGHT as the road passes into the campground parking lot and out the other side.

18.5 Pass through a gate, and after 20 yards, turn RIGHT into the state forest headquarters parking lot, where the tour began.

Additional Information
Otter River State Forest, MA 202, Winchendon, MA (508-939-8962).

Bicycle Service
O'Neil's Bicycle Shop, 108 Main Street, Gardner (508-632-7200). Sales, service.

Wachusett Mountain

Distance: 11.8 miles
Terrain: Dirt and gravel roads, with some pavement; frequent hills with maximum vertical rise of 800 feet
Difficulty: Moderate to difficult
Map: Wachusett Mountain State Reservation (available at visitor center); NEC Wachusett Mountain and Leominster State Forest; USGS 7.5′ × 15′ Wachusett Mountain

Of all the places to ride off-road in eastern Massachusetts, Wachusett is one of the few that gives riders a chance to put the mountain back into mountain biking. Wachusett Mountain is the highest point in Massachusetts east of the Connecticut River, and its slopes are traversed by a network of dirt, gravel and paved roads that provide some of the most sustained climbing of any tour in this book. The effort of this ride pays off, however, as riders who complete the grinding climb to the summit are rewarded by a sweeping 360-degree view across central Massachusetts and into southern New Hampshire and Vermont.

The outstanding view from the summit of Wachusett comes from the commanding place the mountain holds in the surrounding geography. Rising to a height of 2,006 feet, Wachusett towers over the plains and small hills around it. The mountain is what geologists call a monadnock, a free-standing mountain, not part of any range. It was formed 100 million years ago when molten granite was pushed up by the buckling of the earth's crust to form a solitary peak over 23,000 feet high. Rain, wind and four ice ages have eroded 21,000 of those feet, but even so Wachusett still stands out as the most visible landmark in eastern and central Massachusetts.

Wachusett's visibility has always made it a focal point for the people who have lived in its shadow. The Nipmuck Indians recognized the strategic value of the mountain and built a village at its base, giving Wachusett its name, which means "by the great hill." This village was used as a gathering place and base camp for the Indians during King Philip's War in 1675, when several Indian tribes in Massachusetts banded under Chief Metacomet to stop the encroachment of white settlers on their territory. It was also a center of Indian activity during the French and Indian War (1754–1763). Despite these efforts, the Indians were eventually pushed out of the area, and Wachusett and the neighboring town of Princeton were settled, cleared and carved into farmland and pasture.

In the late nineteenth century, the strategic value of Wachusett was again recognized by the people living nearby, this time as a tourist attraction. The town of Princeton became popular as a summer resort area as Bostonians fled the humidity and congestion of the city for the refreshing mountain air of Wachusett. Twelve hotels were built in town, and a road was laid to the mountain's summit in order to make the rarefied air and fine view more accessible by horse and carriage. Soon, a hotel went up at its very top, and although this development destroyed any vestige of wilderness there, the popularity of the mountain led to its eventual salvation. In 1900, a group of citizens who recognized the unique natural beauty of the area pushed the state to purchase the land and preserve it for public use.

The result of this effort was the creation of the Wachusett Mountain State Reservation, a carefully managed, mixed-use recreation area with 20 miles of hiking trails, dirt and gravel roads for mountain biking, a paved automobile road to the summit and a downhill ski area. In order to limit erosion, mountain bikes are not allowed on the hiking trails and are restricted to the dirt, gravel and paved roads. Despite these limitations, there is still a lot of good riding, since many of the dirt and gravel roads are barely more than wide, rough trails. The ride given here circles the mountain along these roads and connects with the paved auto road, which is the only way to reach the summit by bike. Although the riding isn't steep, the roads repeatedly climb and descend in steady grades, providing a strenuous and challenging ride.

To Get There: From MA 2, take the exit for MA 2A and MA 140 South, Westminster, Princeton. Follow MA 140 South for 2.3 miles, then turn right onto Mile Hill Road at the sign for Wachusett Mountain Ski Area and State Park. Follow Mile Hill Road for 1.9 miles, passing the ski area entrance, then turn right at the sign for Wachusett Mountain State Reservation into the parking lot.

The Ride

0.0   The ride begins at the visitor center. From the parking lot entrance, turn LEFT on Mile Hill Road, riding down the hill.

0.7   Just as the ski lodge comes into sight, turn LEFT at a power transformer through a wire gate onto a dirt and gravel road (Balance Rock Road). Follow this road as it climbs across the ski slopes. Be sure to stay on the road and avoid riding on the ski slopes, as they are fragile watershed areas.

If you have skied at Wachusett during the winter, riding along this

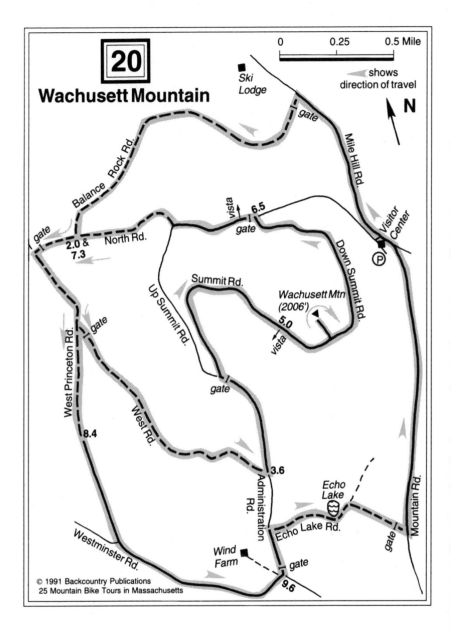

20
Wachusett Mountain

0   0.25   0.5 Mile

shows
direction of travel

N

Ski
Lodge

gate

Mile Hill Rd.

Visitor
Center

Balance Rock Rd.

gate

vista

6.5

gate

North Rd.

**2.0 &
7.3**

P

Summit Rd.

Wachusett Mtn
(2006')

5.0

Down Summit Rd.

Up Summit Rd.

vista

West Princeton Rd.

gate

gate

West Rd.

8.4

3.6

Administration Rd.

Echo
Lake

Mountain Rd.

Westminster Rd.

Wind
Farm

Echo Lake Rd.

gate

gate

9.6

© 1991 Backcountry Publications
25 Mountain Bike Tours in Massachusetts

section of trail may elicit a sense of *déjà vu* as you cross the ski slopes. It is hard to believe that only a few months before these same quiet green meadows were covered with snow and packed with hordes of barely-in-control first-time skiers. Skiing, a sport that many consider to be the spiritual ancestor of mountain biking, has been popular on Wachusett since the 1930's. The Pine Hill Trail, cut by the Civilian Conservation Corps down the steep west face of the mountain, provided a challenging run for skiers willing to hike up the mountain to get their downhill thrills. In the 1960's, a T-bar was built on the north side of the mountain, removing most of the work and some of the fun from the sport. Since then the ski area has been enlarged and developed, and it is a popular destination for day-trippers from Greater Boston. On a mountain bike, struggling to climb to the top of the mountain and then gracefully swooping down, you can recapture the feeling of reward that skiers enjoyed in the days before lifts were built.

2.0   Bear RIGHT as you reach a fork (North Road).

2.2   Pass through a gate and turn LEFT onto a smooth dirt road (West Princeton Road).

2.6   Take your first LEFT and pass through a gate onto a dirt and gravel road (West Road).

3.6   At a T intersection, turn LEFT onto a paved road (Administration Road).

4.2   Pass through a gate and bear RIGHT as you continue on the paved road (Summit Road).

5.0   Take a break from the uphill climb for a view at the overlook on the right. From this vista there is a good view of the Princeton wind farm, the cluster of spinning windmills visible just below you that generate electricity to supplement the town's energy needs.

5.2   Turn LEFT at the sign marked Wachusett Mountain State Reservation Summit.

5.4   You reach the summit area.

With the opening of a road up the mountain in the late 1800's, the summit of Wachusett Mountain became open to development as a summer resort. A three-story hotel was built there, then rebuilt three times, the last being in 1907. The hotel stayed open until the 1940's, and was standing until 1970 when it burned to the ground. The only building still standing on the summit today is Parker Lodge, which was constructed in the 1930's by the Civilian Conservation Corps as a recreation cabin. Today, the lodge is used as a communications center for several state agencies which control the communications towers on top of the mountain.

Despite the less-than-scenic towers, the summit still provides an outstanding 360-degree view. To the north you can see Mount Watatic (14 miles away) and directly behind it Temple Mountain (23 miles away). To the northeast, you have a clear view of the twin cities of Fitchburg and Leominster. In the east, Prospect Hill is visible (33 miles away) and just to its right is the Boston skyline (45 miles away).

Looking west to northwest on a clear day, just on the horizon, you can spot Mount Greylock (65 miles away), Haystack Mountain (60 miles away) and Stratton Mountain (67 miles away). Farther to the northwest is the prominent peak of Mount Monadnock .(26 miles away).

After viewing the summit, head back the way you came.

5.6 At a T intersection, turn LEFT, following the one-way sign, to head down the Summit Road.

6.5 At a T intersection, turn LEFT and pass through an open gate, continuing on the paved road.

Shortly after you make this turn, you have a clear view down the ski slopes to Wachusett Lake. If you enjoy birdwatching, this is a good place for spotting hawks, falcons, osprey and even eagles, as Wachusett lies in the path of a major migration route for birds of prey. During the migration season from October to November, as many as 20,000 birds have been sighted in a single day.

6.8 Take your first RIGHT onto a paved road, which after 30 yards turns into a dirt road (North Road).

7.3 Continue STRAIGHT past another dirt road joining in from the right. At this point you join a section of North Road you were on previously. You will be retracing your earlier tracks for the next 0.6 mile.

7.5 Pass through a gate and turn LEFT onto a smooth dirt road (West Princeton Road). Continue STRAIGHT on this road; do not turn off as you did earlier.

8.4 The road turns to rough pavement.

8.8 Just after passing the Harrington Farm, turn LEFT at a T intersection (Westminster Road).

9.6 As the road you are on turns right, bear LEFT through a gate on a paved road (Administration Road).
The dirt road on your left at this intersection leads up a hill to the Princeton wind farm, which you looked down on earlier. Ride up the hill if you would like a closer look at the windmills.

9.8 Take your first RIGHT onto a dirt road (Echo Lake Road).

10.2 As you pass Echo Lake on your left, stay on the dirt road as it turns to the RIGHT.

10.5 Pass through a gate and turn LEFT at a T intersection onto a paved road (Mountain Road).

11.8 You are back at the visitor center, where the ride began.

Additional Information
Wachusett Mountain State Reservation, Mountain Road, Princeton, MA (508-464-2987). Visitor center open 8:00 a.m. to 4:00 p.m.

Bicycle Service
Gamache Cyclery Inc., 65 Laurel St., Fitchburg (508-343-3140). Sales, service.
Joe's Bicycle Shop, 71 North Main Street, Leominster (508-537-5487). Sales, service.
O'Neil's Bicycle Shop, 38 Main Street, Fitchburg (508-345-0365). Sales, service.

21

Ware River Watershed

Distance: 16.4 miles
Terrain: Flat to rolling dirt road, with some connecting pavement
Difficulty: Easy to moderate
Map: USGS 7.5′ × 15′ Barre

Many people are familiar with Quabbin Reservoir, the 25,000-acre water supply in the center of Massachusetts that quenches the thirst of over a third of the state's population. Fewer, however, know of the Ware River watershed, associated with the Quabbin and also an important source of water for metropolitan Boston. It comprises over 20,000 acres in the towns of Barre, Hubbardston, Oakham and Rutland taken by the MDC in the 1920's when the Ware River was diverted to supplement flow from the Quabbin. This vast area once held houses, schools, stores and factories. When the course of the river was changed, all the buildings were moved or demolished and their occupants relocated in order to protect the purity of the water draining into the river. Today, the watershed is an expansive reservation maintained for limited recreational use by the public. Because the region was once populated, it is crisscrossed by a sprawling network of dirt roads, paths and abandoned railroad beds, ideal avenues for exploration by mountain bike.

The creation of the Ware River watershed was one more controversial chapter in the continuing story of rural Massachusetts towns sacrificed in order to satisfy water demand by the big city. Because it has little surface water, Boston has always had problems getting enough water. From its establishment in 1630 it relied on wells and springs for domestic use. These groundwater sources sufficed for its first 150 years, but by 1795 demand exceeded capacity and an aqueduct was built to bring water from Roxbury's Jamaica Pond into Boston. Since then, each time the city needed water it looked west, searching farther out for sources of clean water. In 1845 Lake Cochituate in Natick was chosen as a reservoir site, and a fourteen-mile aqueduct was constructed to funnel water into the city. In 1872 the Sudbury River and then several lakes in the Framingham area were tapped. Still, by 1893, population growth and industrial development were causing water shortages in Boston and its suburbs. In 1895, work began on the Wachusett Reservoir in Boylston; 40 percent of Boylston's population was relocated and half the town flooded to create the reservoir. But by the time the reservoir was completed in 1908, Boston's population had once again mushroomed and the city's water board was already looking elsewhere for additional supply.

Having exhausted all nearby sources, the state legislature approved a plan in 1926 for the construction of a vast water project in central Massachusetts. This project included diversion of the Ware River, creation of the Quabbin Reservoir in the Swift River Valley, and the laying of an aqueduct to carry the flow east from these two sources. The diversion was completed in 1931, but construction of the Quabbin took much longer because four towns in the Swift River Valley had to be depopulated, buildings removed, trees and brush cleared and dams and dikes built to prepare the reservoir. Filling of the Quabbin began in 1941, but because the city began drawing water immediately it took until 1946 to fill completely. By the time the entire water project was finished, it had cost 60 million dollars and caused 28 deaths, and it had obliterated four entire towns and parts of seven others.

A number of those lost towns were located in the Ware River watershed. Unlike at the Quabbin, where whole villages ended up underwater, there was no flooding at the Ware; the river was simply diverted into the Quabbin aqueduct. However, in order to maintain water quality, the MDC felt it necessary to purchase and protect the hills surrounding the upper Ware valley which form its watershed. The residents of this area fought this decision over seven years of harsh political battles, but their objections were eventually drowned out by stronger voices in the city. When the state appropriated the land, businesses were moved, houses demolished and residents uprooted. In the course of this controversy, property values in the Ware River valley plummeted, and the occupants were not even able to obtain reasonable compensation for their land. Today, all that is left of these lost towns are occasional cellar holes, cemeteries and the memories of their former residents.

This ride follows abandoned dirt roads through the Ware River watershed and past the sites of some of its former villages. Many of these roads are still in good shape, so the riding is generally fast and relatively easy. The roads covered in this tour represent only a fraction of the riding possibilities in the Ware River watershed and its surrounding areas. As you ride you will pass by countless paths, many of them not shown on the map, waiting to be explored by adventuresome mountain bikers.

To Get There: From MA 2, take the exit for MA 68, Hubbardston, Baldwinville. Follow MA 68 South for 9.2 miles, then turn right onto MA 62 West. Follow MA 62 West for 2.2 miles, then turn left onto Rutland Road at the sign for Barre Falls Dam. Follow Rutland Road for 1.1 miles

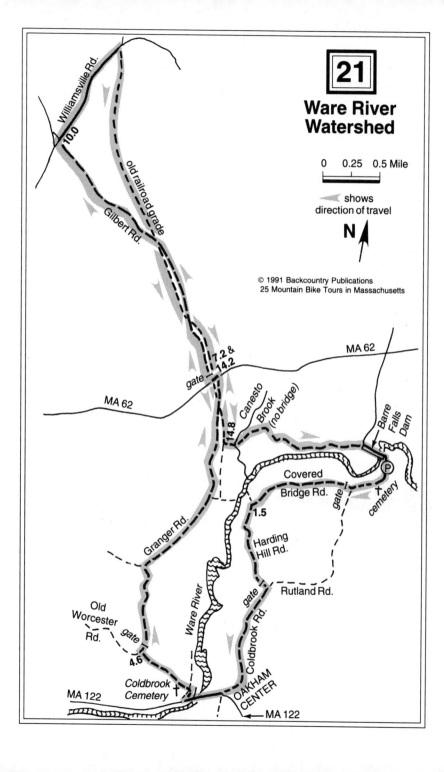

21

Ware River Watershed

0   0.25   0.5 Mile

shows direction of travel

N

© 1991 Backcountry Publications
25 Mountain Bike Tours in Massachusetts

Williamsville Rd.

10.0

old railroad grade

Gilbert Rd.

MA 62

MA 62

7.2 & 14.2

gate

14.8

Canesto Brook (no bridge)

Barre Falls Dam

P

Covered Bridge Rd.

gate

cemetery

Granger Rd.

1.5

Harding Hill Rd.

Rutland Rd.

gate

Coldbrook Rd.

Ware River

Old Worcester Rd.

gate

4.6

Coldbrook Cemetery

OAKHAM CENTER

MA 122

MA 122

across the dam to the picnic area on the left, and park in the spaces provided next to it.

The Ride

0.0 The ride begins from the picnic area at the Barre Falls Dam. Start on the paved road (Rutland Road) which runs past the picnic area, keeping the picnic area to your left.

The 62-foot Barre Falls Dam is part of a system of reservoirs built to control flood waters in the Connecticut River basin. The dam was built in 1958 by the Army Corps of Engineers at a cost of $2,000,000. It is estimated that it would prevent over $4,000,000 worth of damage in the event of a major flood.

0.3 As you pass by an old cemetery on the left, the road turns to dirt.

0.5 At a fork marked by a sign for Ware River Watershed, bear RIGHT and go through a gate (Covered Bridge Road).

1.5 As you reach the bottom of a long hill, bear LEFT at a fork (Harding Hill Road).

2.4 Go though a gate and after 70 yards, at a four-way intersection, turn RIGHT (Coldbrook Road).

3.5 As the dirt road ends at a four-way intersection marked Oakham Center, 3, turn RIGHT onto a paved road (MA 122).

3.8 Just after crossing the river and entering Barre, turn RIGHT onto a dirt road. This will be your second right after crossing the river. The first right is a paved, dead-end road.

4.0 At a five-way intersection, turn LEFT on a dirt road marked by a sign for Ware River Watershed.

4.1 You pass Coldbrook Cemetery on the left.

This cemetery is all that is left of Coldbrook Springs, one of the villages that was destroyed as a result of the Ware River watershed project. Originally an outlying settlement of the town of Oakham, Coldbrook Springs got its start as a village in 1830 when a county road was laid through the site, giving industries access to the Ware River for water power. The Parkers, a prominent family in the area, opened a sawmill on the river about 1850. Other family members started the Oakham and Coldbrook Springs Telephone Company, ran the general store and post office, and served as town officers or state representatives.

In the 1890's, Coldbrook Springs became popular as a resort when vacationers came to enjoy the curative powers of the mineral springs from which the village got its name. Two railroad lines, the

Canesto Brook in the Ware River Watershed

Boston and Albany and the Boston and Maine, had stations in town and several resort hotels were built to cater to the tourist trade. The hotels were in operation until the late 1920's when the land was purchased by the MDC and all the buildings on it were moved or demolished.

4.6 At a T intersection, turn RIGHT, and after 30 yards go through a gate marked by a sign for Ware River Watershed (Old Worcester Road).

5.3 At a T intersection, turn RIGHT (Granger Road).

7.2 As you reach a paved road (MA 62), turn LEFT, and after 30 yards turn RIGHT onto a dirt road (Gilbert Road) and go through a gate marked by a sign for Ware River Watershed.

10.0 As you reach a paved road (Williamsville Road), turn RIGHT.

11.0 Just before reaching a fork marked by a sign for Williamsville Road, Templeton, turn RIGHT onto a wide and straight dirt path, which is an old railroad grade. Continue STRAIGHT on this railroad grade through successive intersections as it crosses back and forth across a dirt road.

14.2 As you reach a paved road (MA 62), cross over and continue STRAIGHT on the railroad grade.

14.4 As you cross a dirt road, bear LEFT to stay on the railroad grade.

14.8 At a four-way intersection, turn LEFT onto a dirt road that runs down a small hill. After 100 yards, at the remains of a stone bridge, continue STRAIGHT across a stream (Canesto Brook). Since the bridge is out, you will have to carry your bike across the steam. It is easiest to cross just to the left of the old bridge.
    If the water level in the stream is too high to cross, you can complete the tour by backtracking along the railroad grade to the last paved road you crossed (MA 62) and following this road east to Rutland Road, where you turn right to reach the Barre Falls Dam.

After crossing the stream, continue STRAIGHT along the dirt road on the other side.

16.2 As you reach a paved road (Rutland Road), turn RIGHT.

16.4 You are back at the Barre Falls Dam picnic area, where the tour began.

Additional Information
Quabbin Visitor Center (MDC), 485 Ware Road, Belchertown, MA (413-323-7221).

Bicycle Service
Country Bike and Sports, 509 Exchange Street, Barre (508-355-2219). Sales, service, rentals.

Holyoke Range

Distance: 18.2 miles
Terrain: Forest trail and dirt path, with 4.5 miles of pavement to return to the start; frequent climbs with a maximum vertical rise of 1,000 feet
Difficulty: Difficult
Map: NEC Holyoke Range State Park Western Section and Eastern Section (available at visitor center); USGS 7.5′ × 15′ Mount Holyoke; USGS 7.5′ × 15′ Belchertown

Rising abruptly from the Connecticut River to heights of over 1,100 feet above sea level, the sinuous spine of the Holyoke Range stands out sharply from the surrounding landscape. When viewed from a distance the range is visually striking. Running in a contrary direction, it is more gracefully arched than the mountains around it, and even when seen at a closer approach, the range maintains its uniqueness. Because the mountains rise so steeply from the floor of the broad, flat Connecticut River Valley, there are expansive views from their cliffs and summits. Within the nine-mile range are over 45 miles of hiking trails and bridle paths that make these vistas easily accessible on a mountain bike. Many of the trails run through the 3,000 acres of land protected by the Holyoke Range and Skinner State Parks, and additional paths cross private land to which public access has been granted. Together, these routes provide mountain bikers with one of the most extensive and challenging trail systems in eastern Massachusetts.

The unique appearance of the Holyoke Range is due to an inexplicable event in the distant geologic past. Formed hundreds of millions of years ago, it is a remnant of a time when New England was covered with active volcanos. Like other mountains in the Connecticut River Valley,

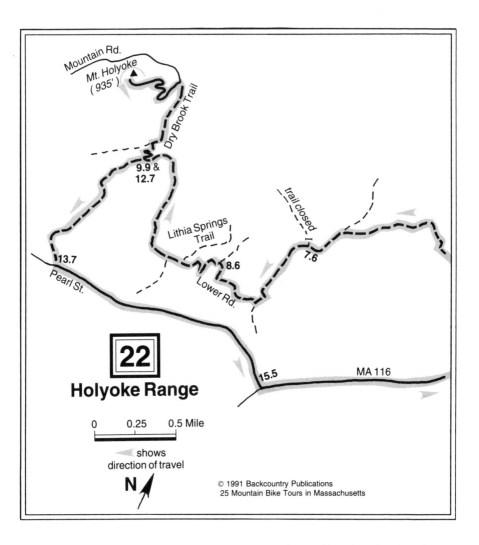

Mountain Rd.

Mt. Holyoke
(935')

Dry Brook Trail

**9.9 &
12.7**

trail closed

Lithia Springs
Trail

8.6

7.6

13.7

Pearl St.

Lower Rd.

22
Holyoke Range

0   0.25   0.5 Mile

shows
direction of travel

N

15.5

MA 116

© 1991 Backcountry Publications
25 Mountain Bike Tours in Massachusetts

the Holyoke Range was created when a vast layer of basalt, or hardened volcanic lava, was uplifted then worn down by erosion and glacial movement over millions of years. For some unknown reason, the Holyoke Range was formed in an east-west direction, while every other range in the valley runs north-south.

The east-west orientation that makes the range geologically unique also make it botanically so, since the range forms the boundary between northern and southern New England forest regions. In northern New England, forests are primarily composed of hemlock, white pine, beech and birch; in southern New England, oak, hickory and shrubs of the

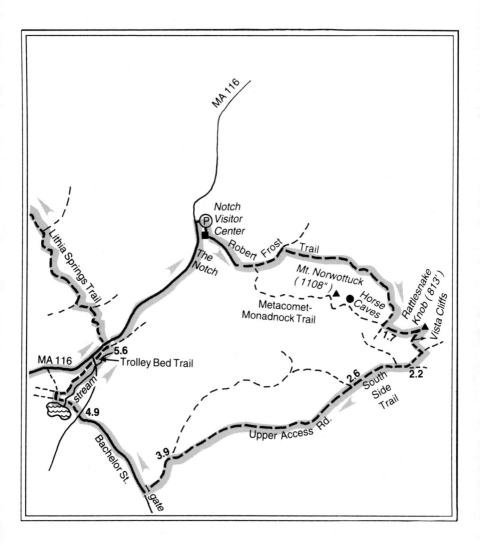

heath family predominate. Generally, the boundary between these two types of forests varies according to local conditions, and is difficult to distinguish. The ridge of the Holyoke Range, however, provides a sharp border. The warm, dry southern side of the range favors southern New England forests, while the cool, dry northern flank supports the northern New England type. By riding through both sides of the range, you get a picture of the diversity of plant life found throughout New England.

This ride follows two briefly connected loops through the Holyoke Range, which is divided down the middle by MA 116: one loop is in the eastern section of the range, and the other in the western. Although many of the trails covered on this ride are wide carriage paths, they are often steep, rocky and challenging. There are frequent long climbs, including one to the summit of Mount Holyoke. This is a long ride and it is important to leave enough time to complete it. If you prefer a shorter ride, it is possible to do just one of these loops. If you opt for the entire ride and run out of time, there are a number of points at which the ride may be shortened by leaving the trails and returning to the start on paved roads.

In order to prevent damage, the trails in the Holyoke Range are closed to mountain bikes when it is raining or when the trails are wet. Please respect these closings so that access to the trails can be continued.

To Get There: From I-91, take exit 19 for MA 9 East. Follow MA 9 East to MA 116 South. Follow MA 116 South for 5.0 miles from the point it splits off from MA 9, then turn left at the sign for the Holyoke Range State Park Notch visitor center into the parking lot.

The Ride

0.0   The ride begins from the visitor center parking lot. Start on the paved path that runs from the parking lot toward the visitor center. After 150 yards, turn RIGHT onto the Robert Frost Trail, which is marked by orange blazes. Continue following the orange blazes as the trail winds through intersecting trails near the visitor center and then begins to climb Mount Norwottuck.

1.7   At a fork marked by signs for Rattlesnake Knob, Mount Norwottuck and the Horse Caves, turn LEFT, following the sign for Rattlesnake Knob up a short, steep hill. Continue following the orange blazes.

A right turn at this intersection onto a white-blazed trail (Metacomet-Monadnock Trail) will bring you to the Horse Caves after 0.3 mile. According to local legend, the Horse Caves were used to hide horses and men during Shays' Rebellion in 1786–1787. The American Revolution was an expensive war, and at its conclusion both the government of Massachusetts and many individual citizens found themselves in considerable debt. The farmers of central and western Massachusetts were especially hard hit, as their farms had run down while they were away fighting. Unable to pay their taxes and meet their debts, their land and livestock were confiscated by the courts in lieu of payment. The farmers viewed this treatment as unfair, and their frustration mounted.

Daniel Shays, a captain of the Revolution and warden of the town of Pelham, decided that action was needed, and he galvanized the disgruntled group of citizens into a rebellion. Fifty western Massachusetts towns sent representatives to a meeting during which a list of grievances was drawn up and presented to the state legislature in Boston. When it failed to address these grievances, the citizens formed a rag-tag army under Shays' command and forced the courts to stop issuing judgments against those in debt. Although the citizens were successful in holding up the courts for a short while, the Massachusetts state militia was called in to put down the rebellion. When Shays' forces tried to take over the Springfield arsenal, they were routed by the better-equipped militia and fled in retreat. The Horse Caves were used as a hiding spot during this retreat by men escaping from the militia as it hunted down those who had taken part in the short-lived rebellion.

2.0   Continue on the orange-blazed trail as in turns sharply to the right past a trail on the left marked Vista.

The trail to the left marked Vista is a spur trail which leads in 100 feet to the top of a cliff with a sweeping view of the eastern end of the Holyoke Range.

2.2   As the orange-blazed trail turns sharply to the left, bear RIGHT onto a trail marked by blue blazes (Southside Trail). After 100 yards, bear LEFT and continue following the blue blazes.

2.6   As the blue-blazed trail turns to the right, bear LEFT onto a wide trail identified by a red triangular horse marker 30 feet down on the right side of the trail. Continue on this trail as it gradually runs downhill.

3.9   Bear LEFT as you join another trail coming down from the right.

4.2   At the end of the trail, pass through a metal gate and turn RIGHT onto a paved road (Bachelor Street).

4.9   Continue STRAIGHT across a paved road onto a dirt road. Continue on this dirt road past a pond on the left.

5.0   After crossing a stream and climbing a small hill, bear RIGHT, and after ten yards, turn RIGHT at a three-way intersection onto a wide, flat dirt path (Trolley Bed Trail).

5.4   Continue STRAIGHT as the trail crosses a paved road.

5.6   As you reach a sign on the left with a yellow dot and an arrow, turn LEFT and cross the paved road (MA 116). After crossing the road, turn LEFT, and in 50 yards turn RIGHT onto a paved road which quickly turns to dirt (Lithia Springs Trail). Continue on this dirt road, following the yellow blazes through successive trail junctions.

If you prefer to end your ride at this point, turn right onto MA 116 and follow it back to the visitor center.

7.6   At an intersection with a road on the right that passes through the remains of a chainlink fence, continue STRAIGHT. You no longer will be following the yellow blazes.

8.2   At a telephone pole marked by a rusted green metal box, turn RIGHT onto a dirt road (Lower Road).

8.6   At a T intersection, turn LEFT.

8.9   As a yellow-blazed trail (Lithia Springs Trail) joins in from the right, continue STRAIGHT, now following the yellow blazes.

9.9   Continue following the yellow-blazed trail as it intersects with a trail joining in from the left and turns sharply to the RIGHT.
    From this point the route climbs very steeply for 0.5 mile up a rough trail to reach the Mount Holyoke auto road, which it follows to the summit of Mount Holyoke. After reaching the summit, it returns to this point. The view from the summit of Mount Holyoke is worth the effort, but if you don't have the time or energy to complete it you can shorten the ride by turning left here and skipping to the directions at mile 12.7. You will have just turned onto the wide dirt path referred to in those directions.

10.0   At a fork, bear RIGHT onto a trail marked by red blazes (Dry Brook Trail).

10.4   The red-blazed trail reaches the paved road running to the summit of Mount Holyoke (Mountain Road). Turn LEFT and follow the paved road to the summit.

11.2   You reach the summit of Mount Holyoke.
    "I have been all over England, have traveled through the highlands of Scotland; I have passed up and down the Rhine. I have ascended Mt. Blanc and stood on Campagna in Rome; but have never seen anything so surprisingly lovely as this." Thus spoke Senator Charles Sumner of Massachusetts in describing the view from the summit of Mount Holyoke in the summer of 1847. In spite of these being the words of a politician describing his home state, they are still high praise and have been echoed many times over by those who have made the pilgrimage to the top of the mountain.
    The first climbers of Mount Holyoke reached the summit in 1676, and a single-room mountain house, the first mountain-top shelter in North America, was built there in 1821. In 1851 the house was expanded into a hotel and for the next 40 years Mount Holyoke thrived as thousands, including Abraham Lincoln and Charles Dickens, climbed the mountain to take in what was called "the most cultivated view in America."
    Although many people were willing to climb Mount Holyoke on foot, in 1854 a primitive lift was constructed up the top half of the mountain to make the visit easier. The "car" itself was made from the

View from the Holyoke Range

backseats of two sleighs nailed together face-to-face. A 600-foot wooden stairway with rails on both sides ran up the steep northwest slope of the mountain, and a horse on the summit provided the power that drew the car up these rails on a rope. The stairs were for those whose nerves were not steady enough to chance a ride in the cable car, and for those times when the rope got wet and shrank, preventing the car from being lowered all the way to the bottom. This rickety means of transport up the mountain lasted until 1867, when the cable car was rebuilt and enclosed, and a steam engine replaced the horses at the top. In 1908 the hotel was expanded and improved with modern plumbing, electricity and an electric tram to bring visitors to the top. The hotel remained open until 1938 when it was severely damaged by a hurricane, then closed until it was restored to its turn-of-the-century appearance and reopened as a historical site in 1988.

The celebrated view from the summit encompasses more than 40 towns and countless mountains in four states, as well as thousands of patchwork acres of cultivated land. One of the most interesting features of the view is the Oxbow, a circular lake that was once part of the Connecticut River. Until 1840 the Connecticut River flowed in a meander around the Oxbow that locals described as "going 3½ miles to gain 30 rods." In 1840, an ice jam in the Oxbow raised the water level in the river until it flowed across the field that separated the two ends of the "bow." In a few hours a new channel had been cut and the course of the river was changed. This event had ramifications for the towns around the river: the people in Northampton celebrated the river's new course, as their journey downriver was now shortened by 3½ miles, but the citizens of Hadley were less pleased, as the river redrew the boundary of their town and they lost 400 acres of land to Northampton.

After viewing the summit, return down on the paved auto road on which you ascended.

12.0   At a sign marked Dry Brook Trail, Rt. 47, 1.5 miles, turn sharply RIGHT onto the red-blazed trail, continuing down the way you came up.

12.5   At an intersection with a yellow-blazed trail (Lithia Springs Trail), turn LEFT to follow the yellow blazes, continuing back the way you came.

12.7   At a T intersection marked by a sign for Lithia Springs Trail, turn RIGHT onto a wide dirt path. You will no longer be following the yellow blazes.

13.7   At the end of the trail, cross over a guardrail and turn LEFT onto a paved road (Pearl Street).

15.5 Turn LEFT onto MA 116 North.
As you reach the top of the hill just before reaching the visitor center, you pass through the Notch, a steep-sided valley cut during the last ice age by a passing glacier. The Notch has always provided the easiest passage through the range, and the road that now runs through it follows the path of an ancient Indian trail that used to extend from Connecticut to Canada. In earlier times the Notch was narrower and more dramatic, but much of the hill that used to form one of its sides has been quarried to provide material for the stone crushing plant you pass on the right.

18.2 You are back at the Holyoke Range State Park Notch visitor center, where the tour began.

Additional Information

Holyoke Range State Park Notch Visitor Center, MA 116, Amherst, MA (413-253-2883).

Skinner State Park, Route 47, Hadley, MA (413-586-0350). Mount Holyoke summit house open weekends mid-May to mid-October.

Friends of the Holyoke Range, 1500 West Street, Amherst, MA 01002.

Bicycle Service

Bicycle World Too, Inc., 63 S. Pleasant Street, Amherst (413-253-7722). Sales, service.

Eastern Mountain Sports, 451 Russell Street, Hadley (413-253-9504). Sales, service.

Peloton, 1 East Pleasant Street, Amherst (413-549-6904). Sales, service.

Valley Bicycle, Ltd., 319 Main Street, Amherst (413-256-0880). Sales, service, rentals.

Metacomet-Monadnock Trail

Distance: 9.3 miles one way; 18.6 miles round trip
Terrain: Rolling to hilly gravel road, dirt path and forest trail
Difficulty: Moderate
Map: Metacomet-Monadnock Trail Guide; USGS 7.5' × 15' Millers Falls; Wendell State Forest (available at state forest headquarters)

Stretching 98 miles across the full length of the state from Connecticut to New Hampshire, the Metacomet-Monadnock Trail is one of the longest continuous hiking corridors in Massachusetts. The trail actually begins in Connecticut, near the Hanging Hills in Meriden, and follows the Connecticut trail system north to the Massachusetts border, crossing near the towns of Agawam and Southwick. From there, it follows a traprock ridge along the west side of the Connecticut River Valley, passing over Provin Mountain, East Mountain and Mount Tom as it meanders through the southern half of the state. About halfway up, the trail turns east, crossing the Connecticut River and tracing the east-west ridge of the Holyoke Range. It then turns north again, climbing Mount Lincoln, Mount Orient, Northfield Mountain and Mount Grace on its way toward the New Hampshire border. After crossing the state line, it reaches its terminus atop Mount Monadnock, where it connects with the Monadnock-Sunapee greenway in New Hampshire. Together, these two trails form a continuous pathway more than 200 miles long.

The Metacomet-Monadnock trail was conceived in the early 1950's by Professor Walter Banfield of the University of Massachusetts at Amherst in response to requests by Connecticut hikers to extend their existing trail system into Massachusetts. Professor Banfield combined resources from the Appalachian Mountain Club, Green Mountain Club and University of Massachusetts Faculty Outing Club to design, lay out and mark the trail. In most cases the trail connected existing paths and carriage roads, taking advantage of state parks, forests and local conservation land along its route.

This ride follows a section of the trail which runs from North Leverett up to and through the Wendell State Forest. The directions given here are for a one-way tour, which requires spotting a car at the endpoint in Wendell State Forest. If you prefer a longer ride or want to avoid spotting a car, it's possible to ride the trail up and back in a full, but not unreasonably long, day. Another alternative is to start the tour in the middle, at Ruggles Pond in Wendell State Forest, and ride one half or the other out and back. The first half of the ride, from North Leverett to Wendell State Forest, is easier, running along dirt roads much of the way. The second half, through Wendell State Forest, is harder but more scenic, following a combination of forest trail and dirt road. On a hot day, swimming is possible at Ruggles Pond in Wendell State Forest and at Mormon Hollow Brook, near the ride's endpoint.

The Metacomet-Monadnock Trail is marked the entire way by rectangular white paint blazes, though at some points there is a considerable distance between them. When following this ride it's helpful to take along a copy of the Metacomet-Monadnock Trail Guide, which includes relevant sections of the USGS maps of the route.

Besides the ride given here, other sections of the Metacomet-Monadnock Trail present intriguing mountain biking possibilities. Since the trail was designed for hikers, some parts may be unrideable, but other sections, particularly where the trail was routed along dirt roads and carriage paths, have prime off-road riding potential. The trail guide can offer insight into which sections might provide good riding. Be aware, however, that the bridge over the Millers River, which the trail is supposed to cross in passing from Farley to MA 2 just north of the ride given here, has been washed out and getting around it requires a 16-mile detour. It is also possible that other sections of the trail described in the guidebook have been rerouted. If you attempt to ride any uncharted segments of the trail, be sure to investigate alternate trails before you start in case the route you are planning to follow is impassable. Also, please remember to observe the IMBA guidelines for courteous riding, especially on parts of the trail where you are likely to encounter hikers or horseback riders.

To Get There: To get to the start of the ride, from MA 2 take MA 63 South toward Millers Falls. Follow MA 63 South for 5.1 miles, then turn left onto North Leverett Road, which is opposite signs on the right for MA 47 South. Follow North Leverett Road for 2.1 miles into the town of North Leverett and park in the lot beside the large white North Leverett Baptist church on the left.

To get to the end of the ride to spot a car, from MA 2 take MA 63 South for 0.3 mile toward Millers Falls. At an intersection in the town of Millers Falls where MA 63 turns right, continue straight on Wendell Road, following the sign for Wendell State Forest. Continue straight across a metal bridge and bear left, still following the sign for Wendell State Forest. After 1.3 miles, bear left at a fork onto Mormon Hollow Road (you will no longer be following the sign for Wendell State Forest). Follow Mormon Hollow Road for 3.9 miles, then at the bottom of a small hill just

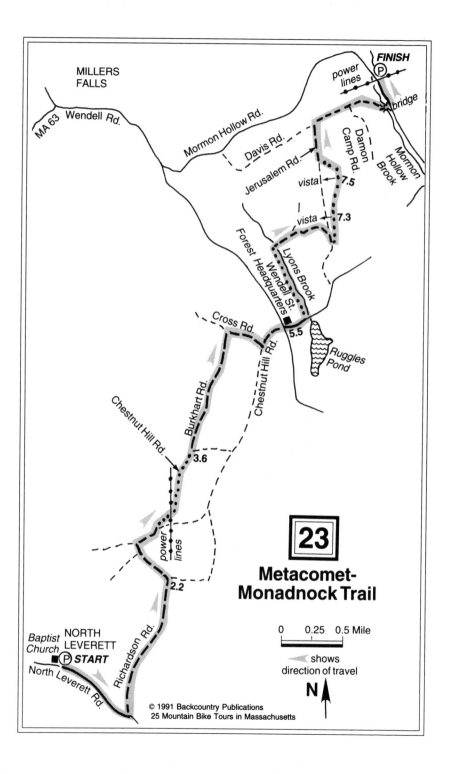

MILLERS
FALLS

MA 63 Wendell Rd.

Mormon Hollow Rd.

Davis Rd.

Jerusalem Rd.

FINISH

power
lines

bridge

Damon Camp Rd.

Mormon Hollow Brook

vista → **7.5**

vista → **7.3**

Lyons Brook

Forest Headquarters

Wendell St.

Cross Rd.

5.5

Ruggles Pond

Chestnut Hill Rd.

Burkhart Rd.

Chestnut Hill Rd.

Chestnut Hill Rd.

3.6

power
lines

23

**Metacomet-
Monadnock Trail**

2.2

Baptist
Church NORTH
LEVERETT
P **START**

North Leverett Rd.

Richardson Rd.

0   0.25   0.5 Mile

◄ shows
direction of travel

N

© 1991 Backcountry Publications
25 Mountain Bike Tours in Massachusetts

after a set of power lines crosses the road overhead, turn left into a dirt parking lot, which is the endpoint of the ride.

The Ride

0.0 The ride starts from the church parking lot. From the parking lot, turn LEFT onto North Leverett Road.

0.8 Turn LEFT onto a dirt road, Richardson Road. At this point you join up with the Metacomet-Monadnock Trail, which is marked by white rectangular paint blazes. You will see the first white blaze on your right as you turn onto Richardson Road. For the rest of the ride, you will be following these white blazes.

1.7 Continue STRAIGHT as the road narrows and moves into the woods.

2.1 Bear RIGHT as another dirt road joins in from the left.

2.2 At a T intersection, turn LEFT.

2.6 At a four-way intersection, turn RIGHT (Chestnut Hill Road).

3.0 As you approach power lines running overhead, turn LEFT on a dirt path that runs under the power lines.

3.1 At a sign marked M and M Trail, turn RIGHT and then immediately LEFT onto dirt path that runs through the woods roughly parallel to the power lines. Continue on this trail, following the white blazes.

3.6 At a fork, bear LEFT on a dirt road (Burkhart Road). Continue following the white blazes as the trail curves right and merges with a road (Cross Road) joining in from the left.

5.2 At a T intersection, turn LEFT (Chestnut Hill Road).

5.5 You reach a paved road (Wendell Road) with the Wendell State Forest headquarters across the road to the left. Continue STRAIGHT across this road onto the paved road that runs into the forest.

The town of Wendell is one of the hilliest towns in central Massachusetts. Settled in 1754, it was incorporated in 1871 and named after Judge Oliver Wendell of Boston, who owned much land in the town and belonged to the same family that produced the famed jurist, Oliver Wendell Holmes. Wendell State Forest, which covers 7,566 acres, takes up much of the town's land area. The forest, large areas of which were burned early in the century, was purchased by the state in the 1920's and improved by the Civilian Conservation Corps in the 1930's. Hilly, with elevations ranging from 800 to 1,100 feet, the forest has two ponds open for fishing, swimming and boating, and over 20 miles of dirt roads and hiking trails.

Metacomet-Monadnock Trail

5.7 As you reach Ruggles Pond on the right, turn LEFT into the parking lot opposite the pond. At the end of the parking lot, bear RIGHT onto a narrow dirt trail marked by a sign for the Metacomet-Monadnock Trail. Follow the white blazes to continue on this trail as it descends beside a stream, crosses the stream and climbs through the woods.

6.7 At the end of the trail, turn RIGHT onto a dirt road.

7.1 At a T intersection, turn RIGHT on a gravel road (Jerusalem Road).

7.2 Following the white blazes, turn LEFT on a narrow trail that climbs steeply up a ridge. You will have to carry your bike for the first 150 yards of this trail. At the top of the ridge, follow the white blazes as the trail turns LEFT and runs along the top of the ridge.

7.3 Continue STRAIGHT past a trail leading off to the left.
The trail leading off to the left is a spur trail that in 100 yards leads to the top of a ledge with good views of the valley below.

7.5 At a T intersection, turn RIGHT. Continue following the white blazes as the trail descends the ridge.
The trail to the left at this intersection brings you to another fine scenic view.

7.6 At the end of the trail, turn RIGHT on a gravel road (Jerusalem Road).

8.2 At a T intersection, turn RIGHT on another gravel road called Davis Road.

8.6 As the gravel road turns RIGHT and becomes Damon Camp Road, continue STRAIGHT on a grassy path. Continue on this path as it runs downhill.

9.0 Just after crossing a wooden bridge over a stream (Mormon Hollow Brook), turn LEFT following the white blazes onto a narrow trail that runs beside the stream. In a short distance, as you pass by the remains of a large stone structure, you may have to cross and recross the stream to stay on the trail, which runs just alongside the stream.
The stone ruins you pass along this section of the trail are the remnants of Mormon Hollow, a Mormon settlement dating from the 1830's.

9.2 As the trail reaches a paved road, turn LEFT onto the road (Mormon Hollow Road).

9.3 Turn RIGHT on a dirt road into a parking area underneath a set of power lines. This is the end of the ride.
From the parking lot where the ride ends, the Metacomet-Monadnock Trail continues on a trail that runs down to and then alongside a stream (Mormon Hollow Brook). This part of the trail is difficult to

ride but worth exploring on foot or by bike since the shallow, slow-moving stream is an inviting place to swim. However, do not plan on following the Metacomet-Monadnock Trail more than a mile or so past this point, as the bridge the trail is supposed to cross over the Millers River has been washed out and a 16-mile detour is required to continue further.

Additional Information

Wendell State Forest, Wendell Road, Millers Falls, MA (413-659-3797).

Metacomet-Monadnock Trail Guide, Seventh Ed., 1991, Berkshire Chapter, Appalachian Mountain Club (distributed by New England Cartographics). Available at the Appalachian Mountain Club, Eastern Mountain Sports in Boston, and bookstores and outdoor stores in the Connecticut River Valley — or by mail from New England Cartographics (see introduction).

Bicycle Service

Bicycle World, 104 Federal Street, Greenfield (413-774-3701).

Peloton Inc., 91 Main Street, Greenfield (413-773-5572).

Mount Toby

Distance: 12.2 miles
Terrain: Bridle path and forest trail, with some connecting pavement; long, frequent climbs with maximum vertical rise of 1,000 feet
Difficulty: Difficult
Map: NEC Mount Toby; USGS 7.5′ × 15′ Mt. Toby

It seems as if every mountain in Massachusetts has had a hotel built on its summit at one point or another, and Mount Toby is no exception. Even as early as the 1870's the mountain was a popular summer resort with a hotel and observation tower at the top. Although the hotel and tower are long gone, the roads that brought carriages of tourists to the summit are still there. Today, these old carriage roads, now wide dirt paths, provide a perfect route for climbing to the top of the mountain by bike. However, they don't make the trip easy — the five miles of sustained climbing on this ride will tax the ability of all but the most fit riders.

Although tough by bike, the climb to the summit must have been even more difficult for Captain Elnathan Toby, said to have been the first white settler to reach the top of the mountain. Captain Toby had come to the area to protect the local settlers from Indian attacks, and he climbed the mountain to scout the surrounding countryside. The Indians who lived there believed that the steep-sided summit was home to evil spirits, and many battles took place on the mountain between the Indians and the early settlers. In later years, the Indians sold the mountain and surrounding land to the white settlers for 80 fathoms of wampum.

In the 1840's, residents of the area again engaged in a fight over the mountain, but this time of a different sort. By that time, Mount Toby had become a popular locale for field trips by students from nearby Amherst College. Edward Hitchcock, then president of Amherst, decided that the mountain needed a more euphonious title and renamed it Metawampe. However, Hitchcock did not bother to consult the local residents, and his attempt to impose the new name on the mountain set off a town-gown battle. In response to Hitchcock's declaration, residents of Sunderland passed a resolution condemning his academic snobbery, and the name of Mount Toby stuck.

Despite the controversy between the town and the college, Toby remained a popular place to visit for students of botany and geology. Because of the variety of its topography and its location on the border between northern and southern New England forest regions, the mountain is an area of exceptional botanical diversity. Oak, birch, beech, maple, hickory, hemlock, pine, ash, basswood, and elm forests grow on the mountain, 42 of the 45 types of ferns growing in the region have been identified there, and a wide variety of orchids bloom on its slopes. It was the mountain's value as a field laboratory that motivated the Massachusetts Agricultural College to purchase over 700 acres of land around it in 1916. Additional land acquisitions since then have increased the reservation's area to 1,100 acres. The college, today the University of Massachusetts, still controls the land and maintains it for field work by students in forestry and other departments.

This ride follows a route that winds circuitously around Mount Toby in order to approach and descend the steep summit cone on the old carriage road, which is the only bikeable way to the top. If you are looking for a shortcut up or down the mountain, use caution, as the other trails to the summit are extremely steep. Some of the trails you will follow on this ride are on private land to which public access has been granted. Please respect this private property and stay on the trails at all times.

To Get There: From I-91, take exit 19 for MA 9 East. Follow MA 9 East, then turn left onto MA 116 North. Follow MA 116 North for 7.1 miles, then turn right on North Silver Lane (2.5 miles from the Sunderland border). Follow North Silver Lane, bearing right at the fork, for 1.2 miles, then turn right onto Park Road. Follow Park Road for 0.4 mile, then park in the parking area on your right, just past a pond.

The Ride

0.0   The ride begins at the parking area on Park Road. Start down Park Road, keeping the pond and the parking area to your right. In a short distance the paved road runs into a dirt path marked by red blazes (North Mountain Road). Continue STRAIGHT on this path, following the red blazes.

1.7   One-tenth of a mile after passing under a set of power lines, turn LEFT on a path marked by blue blazes (Sugar Farms Trail). Watch for the power lines, as there are other blue-blazed trails leading off to the left before this one. Continue on this trail, following the blue blazes.

2.7   Just after crossing a small stream on a wood-plank bridge, bear RIGHT at a fork and continue following the blue blazes.

3.9   The blue-blazed trail ends at a wide dirt road with a metal gate on the left. Turn RIGHT, and continue on this dirt road, following the orange blazes (Robert Frost Trail).

Along this trail you might catch glimpses of Cranberry Pond through the trees on your left. In the 1870's, ice was cut from this pond in winter and stored in an ice house on the mountain's summit. Cool ice

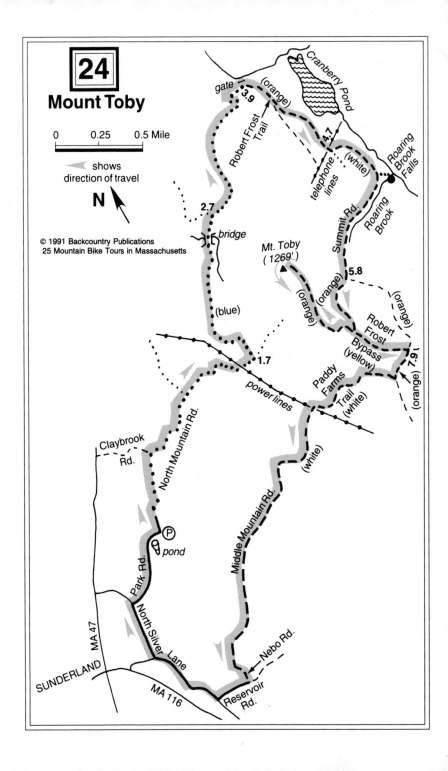

24

Mount Toby

0   0.25   0.5 Mile

shows
direction of travel

N

© 1991 Backcountry Publications
25 Mountain Bike Tours in Massachusetts

Cranberry Pond

gate

3.9

(orange)

Robert Frost Trail

4.7

telephone lines

(white)

Roaring Brook Falls

2.7

Summit Rd.

Roaring Brook

bridge

Mt. Toby
(1269')

5.8

(orange)

(orange)

(orange)

Robert Frost Bypass (yellow)

(blue)

7.9

(orange)

1.7

power lines

Paddy Farms Trail (white)

Claybrook Rd.

North Mountain Rd.

(white)

P

pond

Middle Mountain Rd.

Park Rd.

North Silver Lane

Nebo Rd.

MA 47

SUNDERLAND

MA 116

Reservoir Rd.

water was sold to thirsty tourists for ten cents a glass, an exorbitant price for those times. Today, if you want a cool drink at the top of the mountain, you'll have to bring your own.

4.7   As the orange-blazed trail turns right under telephone lines, bear LEFT to stay on the wide dirt road, now marked with white blazes. Continue following the white blazes (Summit Road).

As the trail meets up with a stream, Roaring Brook, a spur trail leads to the left down to Roaring Brook Falls. In the 1870's, the falls were a popular gathering spot for crowds that would come on weekends to listen to religious sermons. A path was built up the side of the falls, a bridge crossed the stream above them and a fountain was built beside the falls and filled with goldfish. If you want to take a look at the falls, it is best to leave your bike safely hidden on the trail and walk down the steep trail.

5.8   The white blazes marking the road you are on change to orange as you rejoin the orange-blazed trail. Continue STRAIGHT on the wide dirt road, now following the orange blazes.

6.8   You reach the summit of Mount Toby.

The observation tower on the summit, which provides 50-mile views in each direction, is not the first structure to cap the mountain. In the early 1870's, a six-story hotel and tower were constructed and tourists came to Mount Toby from throughout the Connecticut River Valley via the Central Vermont Railroad, which had a station at the base of the mountain near the start of the summit road. From the station, a horse-drawn bus took visitors up the carriage road to the summit hotel, where they could enjoy the view from an observatory in the enclosed tower. Although the mountain remained popular for some time, the hotel had been up for only one year when it burned to the ground. After the fire, rumors circulated that it had been set by a group of puritanical local women who did not approve of the wild "goings-on" at the resort.

After taking in the view from the summit, start back down the way you came up, following the orange-blazed path. Be sure not to take the continuation of the orange-blazed trail which leaves from the opposite side of the summit area.

7.5   As the orange-blazed path you are on turns sharply to the left, turn RIGHT onto a trail marked by yellow blazes (Robert Frost Bypass).

7.9   The yellow-blazed trail you are on joins an orange-blazed trail (Robert Frost Trail). Continue STRAIGHT, now following the orange blazes.

8.0   As the main path continues straight, turn RIGHT onto a narrow trail that runs down a steep embankment, continuing to follow the orange blazes.

8.1   As the orange-blazed trail turns sharply to the left, continue STRAIGHT on the main trail, now marked by white blazes (Paddy Farms Trail to Middle Mountain Road). Continue following the white blazes as the trail descends the flanks of the mountain.

10.6   The dirt road turns to pavement (Nebo Road). After 100 yards, at the end of the road, turn RIGHT (Reservoir Road).

10.9   At the end of the road, turn RIGHT (North Silver Lane).

11.3   At a fork, bear RIGHT.

11.7   Turn RIGHT onto Park Road.

12.2   You are back at the parking area, where the tour began.

Bicycle Service
Bicycle World, 104 Federal Street, Greenfield (413-774-3701). Sales, service.

Northfield Mountain

Distance: 9.3 miles
Terrain: Dirt, grass and gravel path; long, frequent climbs, with maximum vertical rise of 860 feet
Difficulty: Moderate to difficult
Map: Northfield Mountain (available at visitor center); USGS 7.5′ × 15′ Northfield

As the sport of mountain biking grows in popularity, it is likely that we will begin to see the creation of mountain bike parks, recreation areas that cater specifically to off-road riders. Riding at Northfield Mountain, where Northeast Utilities has created one of the best and most carefully managed mountain biking areas in the state, gives you a picture of what such a place might be like. Northfield is a cross country ski area that has opened its excellent trail network to mountain bikes. Like many ski areas, Northfield has realized that mountain biking and cross country skiing are naturally complementary sports: trails that are good for one are generally good for the other, and their seasons do not overlap. Although the trails at Northfield were not designed with mountain biking in mind, they could have been. Wide, graded and practically rock-free paths climb and descend the slopes of 1,095-foot Northfield Mountain, providing strenuous climbs to the summit and smooth downhill runs back to the base.

The trail network at Northfield Mountain is part of the Northfield Mountain Recreation Area, developed and managed by Northeast Utilities, which has built a pumped-storage hydroelectric station in and on the mountain. As a public service, they have also developed the mountain as a recreation and environmental study area that includes self-guided nature trails, interpretive riverboat tours, guided bus tours to the generating station, an exercise course, an orienteering course, picnic area, campgrounds and a cross country ski center. All activities except the riverboat tours are free of charge.

Mountain biking at Northfield Mountain is also free of charge, but before you ride you must register at the visitor center. Northfield's approach to managing the use of bikes on their trail system is very well conceived. They have clearly designated all trails that are open to mountain bikes, they educate riders on safe riding technique and they are carefully monitoring the impact of mountain bikes on the trails by registering all riders. Registration is free and takes only a few minutes.

When you register, you are given a tag that attaches to your bike and has a handy trail map on the back showing the trails on which you are allowed to ride. You are also familiarized with Northfield's mountain biking regulations, which include the requirement to wear an ANSI−or Snell−approved helmet and to uphold the following mountain bike code:

Northfield Mountain Bike Cyclist's Code

1. I will yield the right of way to non-motorized recreationists.

2. I will slow down, use caution and make my presence known well in advance of another person.

3. I will maintain control of speed at all times and approach turns in anticipation of someone around the bend.

4. I will stay on designated ski trails and obey all trail signs.

5. I will respect public and private property.

6. I will come to a full stop at intersections on Reservoir Road.

7. I realize that there may be maintenance and equipment, and workers on the trails at any time.

8. I will respect the closing of trails as posted for any reason deemed necessary by Northfield Mountain.

9. I will anticipate that the gate on Reservoir Road be closed at all times.

10. Reservoir Road is not to be used for ascent or descent except in case of emergency or extreme fatigue, or for crossing from trail to trail.

Mountain biking is allowed on most of the cross country ski trails at Northfield, except for a few of the steepest, which are off limits. In addition, riding is not allowed on the hiking trails or on the paved Reservoir Road. The entire trail system may also be closed at times due to wet weather or maintenance work at the generating station, so it is advisable to call ahead to ensure that the trails are open.

This ride completes a circuit of the Northfield trail network, climbing steadily up one flank of the mountain and then descending the other side almost to the base. It then climbs again on trails that cross the face of the mountain before returning down to the starting point. All of the trails on this ride are wide, smooth and easy to ride, but there is considerable climbing, with some steep sections. If you are accustomed to riding hills this will be an easy tour; if not, it will be a significant challenge. For an easier ride, stay on the trails near the base of the mountain, which offer fun riding without the climbs.

To Get There: From I-91, take exit 28 for Northfield, MA 10 North. Follow MA 10 for 4.4 miles, then turn right onto MA 63 South, following the sign for Northfield Mountain Recreation Area. Continue south on MA 63 for 5.2 miles, then turn left at the sign for Northfield Mountain and follow signs to the parking lot by the visitor center.

The Ride

0.0 The ride begins from the grassy area next to the wooden deck behind the visitor center. Start on the Jug End Trail, marked by signs, that leads from the visitor center across a field and begins to climb through the woods.

0.4 At a three-way intersection marked by signs for the B-Bar-W and Cedar Circuit trails, bear LEFT to stay on the Jug End Trail.

0.6 At trail junction 6A, turn RIGHT onto the 10th Mountain Trail as it begins to climb steeply underneath a set of power lines.

1.4 At trail junction 27, bear RIGHT to stay on the 10th Mountain Trail.

2.5 At trail junction 31, bear RIGHT to stay on the 10th Mountain Trail.

2.7 At trail junction 32, turn RIGHT onto an unnamed spur trail marked by a green circle/easiest sign. As you reach a paved road, turn RIGHT and walk (do not ride) along the edge of the road. After 50 yards bear RIGHT onto a trail marked by a sign for the Reservoir Viewing Platform.

2.9 You reach the reservoir viewing platform.

The 300-acre reservoir at the top of Northfield Mountain was built as part of a pumped-storage generating station located inside the mountain. Work on this station was begun in 1968 as one of a number of energy projects designed to meet the growing demand for power in the region. Northfield Mountain was selected as a site for a pumped-storage hydroelectric facility because of its proximity to the Connecticut River and the natural depression on its summit that provided an ideal location for a high-altitude reservoir. To construct the station, dams and dikes were built on top of the mountain to contain water in the reservoir. Inside the mountain, a cavern 300 feet long and 120 feet high was carved out for the powerhouse and several tunnels were drilled through the mountain to bring water from the reservoir to the powerhouse.

This pumped-storage facility is used to generate supplemental electricity during times of peak demand. At night and on weekends, when power consumption is low, electricity from nearby generating stations is transmitted to Northfield where it is used to run four giant pump/turbines in the powerhouse which pump water diverted from the Connecticut River up to the reservoir. During the day, when

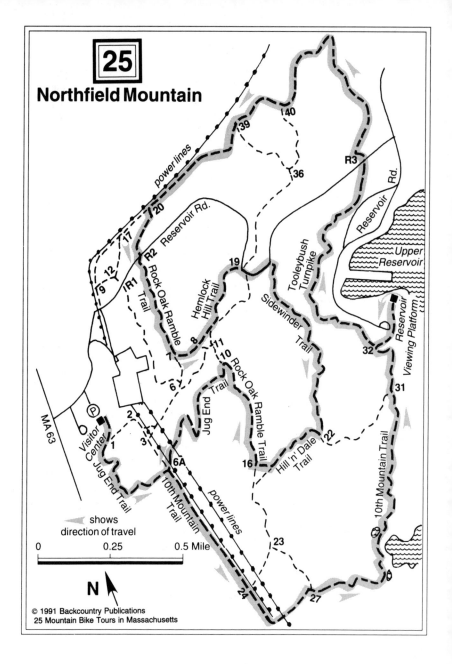

25
Northfield Mountain

extra power is needed to meet peak demand, the water is allowed to flow down a 30-foot-wide shaft to the powerhouse, where it turns the pump/turbines, now to produce electricity. After passing through the powerhouse, the water flows back into the Connecticut River.

The Northfield Mountain pumped-storage facility is capable of generating 1,000,000 kilowatts of electricity. Because it is built inside the mountain and burns no polluting fuel, the station has little impact on the environment and its presence is hardly noticed when riding. If you would like to learn more about the pumped-storage facility, Northeast Utilities runs bus tours to the reservoir and powerhouse from the visitor center.

After viewing the reservoir, return back the way you came to trail junction 32.

3.1   At trail junction 32, turn RIGHT onto the Tooleybush Turnpike.

4.0   As you reach a paved road (Reservoir Road), come to a full stop, cross over and continue STRAIGHT on the other side to stay on the Tooleybush Turnpike as it begins to descend.

At points along this section of trail where the trees open up you get a clear view of the Connecticut River Valley. Look down into the valley and try to imagine how it might have appeared millions of years ago when it was a broad, flat swamp inhabited by giant prehistoric reptiles. Although you may not think of dinosaurs as native to Massachusetts, there is evidence that dinosaurs lived in the Connecticut Valley 190 million years ago; their footprints are still found in the bedrock around Northfield.

Long before the river had formed, the Connecticut Valley was covered with a muddy sediment. Dinosaurs grazing in the valley left footprints, and as the mud hardened the footprints were preserved. The first local dinosaur footprint was discovered in 1802, when a farmer in South Hadley dug up a giant print while plowing and brought it to the attention of local scientists. At the time, no one knew what kind of animal had made the footprint and most scientists thought it had been made by a giant prehistoric bird. Subsequent quarrying in the towns around Northfield uncovered prints in several locations. One site in Gill, known as the "bird track quarry," was mined for footprints for more than 20 years and attracted the interest of scientists from all over the world. It was not until 1859, however, that the tracks were identified as belonging to dinosaurs that lived during the Triassic period, smaller ancestors of the larger, more well-known reptiles of the Jurassic period.

4.9   At trail junction 40, turn RIGHT to stay on the Tooleybush Turnpike.

5.5   At trail junction 20, turn LEFT onto the Rock Oak Ramble Trail. Watch out for this turn, as the trail sign is hidden in the bushes on the right side of the trail.

5.7 As you reach a paved road (Reservoir Road), come to a full stop, cross over and continue STRAIGHT on the other side to stay on the Rock Oak Ramble Trail.

6.1 At trail junction 7, bear LEFT onto the Hemlock Hill Trail and begin to climb again.

6.2 At trail junction 8, bear LEFT at a fork to stay on the Hemlock Hill Trail.

6.6 At trail junction 19, turn RIGHT along the side of the paved road. After a few hundred yards, turn RIGHT onto the Sidewinder Trail.

7.4 At trail junction 22, turn RIGHT onto the Hill 'n' Dale Trail, which descends steeply.

7.6 At trail junction 16, turn RIGHT onto the Rock Oak Ramble Trail.

8.2 At trail junction 10, turn LEFT onto the Jug End Trail.

8.8 At trail junction 6A, continue STRAIGHT to stay on the Jug End Trail. Follow the Jug End Trail back the way you came until you reach the visitor center.

9.3 You are back at the visitor center, where the tour began.

Additional Information
Northfield Mountain Recreation and Environmental Center, Route 63, Northfield, MA (413-659-3713, 413-659-3714). Visitor center open Wednesday through Sunday, 9:00 a.m to 5:00 p.m.

Bicycle Service
The Bicycle Barn, 56 Main Street, Northfield (413-498-2996). Sales, service, rentals.

Also from Backcountry Publications and Countryman Press

Regional Bicycling Guides

30 Bicycle Tours in Wisconsin
25 Bicycle Tours in Ohio's Western Reserve
25 Bicycle Tours in Maryland
25 Bicycle Tours on Delmarva
25 Bicycle Tours in and around Washington, D.C.
25 Bicycle Tours in New Jersey
25 Bicycle Tours in Eastern Pennsylvania
20 Bicycle Tours in the Adirondacks
25 Bicycle Tours in the Hudson Valley
30 Bicycle Tours in New Hampshire
25 Bicycle Tours in Vermont
25 Bicycle Tours in Maine
25 Mountain Bike Tours in Vermont

Other Outdoor Books on Massachusetts and vicinity

50 Hikes in Massachusetts
50 Hikes in Vermont
50 Hikes in the White Mountains
50 Hikes in Connecticut
50 More Hikes in New Hampshire
Canoeing Massachusetts, Rhode Island and Connecticut
Covered Bridges of Vermont
Massachusetts: An Explorer's Guide
Cape Cod and the Islands: An Explorer's Guide
Walks & Rambles on Cape Cod and the Islands
Backwoods Ethics
Wilderness Ethics

We offer many more books on hiking, walking, fishing, and canoeing in New England, New York State—and many more books on travel, nature, and other subjects.

Our books are available at bookstores, or they may be ordered directly from the publisher. For ordering information or for a complete catalog, please contact:

The Countryman Press
c/o W.W. Norton & Company, Inc.
800 Keystone Industrial Park
Scranton, PA 18512
http://web.wwnorton.com